MW00616231

DATE DUE

TH⋯F
LU⋯RY

to ⋯nt

NORTHWESTERN PUBLISHING HOUSE
Milwaukee, Wisconsin

Second printing—January 1994

Library of Congress Card 92-61237
Northwestern Publishing House
1250 N. 113th St., Milwaukee, WI 53226-3284
© 1993 by Northwestern Publishing House.
Published 1993
Printed in the United States of America
ISBN 0-8100-0436-4

To my parents
Bob and June Koester

CONTENTS

PREFACE

Change is a part of life. Styles change, people change, and so do churches and entire church bodies. A hundred years ago many Lutheran churches in America still held German services and families went to church in horse-drawn buggies. But that has changed with the passing years. At the same time, orthodox Christians recognize that God's Word is changeless and the message of the church must always remain the same.

Aware of these realities, we need to ask, "What is the link between what I do and what I believe?" In other words, if we are going to change our way of doing things, how are we to know what changes to make and when to make them—without affecting what we believe? And if we change our methods, what is the fulcrum, or set of principles, we should use to shift our methods from our parents' generation to our own?

All of this raises yet another question: "When does a change in methodology put strains on our theology and result in inadvertent changes to our beliefs?" Or, to put it a little differently, "How can we change our methods while remaining faithful to our theology?"

During the past couple of decades the Church Growth school of thought has been having a tremendous influence on Lutheranism. It's brought changes.

Many Lutheran pastors, particularly in the Lutheran Church—Missouri Synod have delved deeply into Church Growth thought. In the past fifteen years or so, my own

Synod, the Wisconsin Evangelical Lutheran Synod, has worked with Church Growth ideas, always within the context of trying to "Lutheranize" them. But there hasn't been a lot of grass roots theological analysis of Church Growth methods or of our methods in general. Too often, what happens is that theology is stated clearly and methods are stated equally clearly, while the bridge between them remains unconstructed.

I began the work of trying to understand Church Growth thought as a parish pastor. That is what I am at the writing of this book. As all parish pastors, I have been offered many methods to use in evangelism and outreach. Over the years, it has been my growing conviction that if I were ever to come to grips with these methods, I would have to do some work on building the bridge between theology and methodology. Only then could I use the good, and in good conscience set the rest aside.

The bridge had to be built within the context of Lutheran theology. That is what this book is about. It is an attempt to wrestle with methodology from a scriptural and Lutheran standpoint. It is an attempt to understand the truth that methods are not neutral on all levels, but on many levels what we do flows from our theological positions. I hope this will stimulate others to wrestle with these issues. I thank the friends who have given me writings and thoughts which have led me to refine my own.

The reader should realize from the start that I do not consider myself a proponent or a part of the Church Growth Movement. I attended sessions at Fuller Seminary, including Church Growth I and II, in order better to understand this movement that was having such an impact on the world. I have used the opportunity for study afforded by Fuller's Doctor of Ministry program to sharpen my focus on the ministry, and to work through those principles I learned in my seminary training—now with several years in the ministry behind me.

Most importantly, I have tried to analyze what the Bible says about the gospel message, and apply this as rigorously as possible to the work I am doing, letting the gospel itself determine its own methods. The bulk of this book is devoted to working with the gospel, showing the different uses of the word "gospel" in the religious world today, and analyzing which mindsets and methods best reflect the correct understanding of the gospel.

We are all different people. We have different pasts, different "filters" through which we view the world and judge the words and actions of others. Indeed, we ourselves change throughout our lives, growing through past experiences, changing as new positions and demands are placed on us, and growing to understand our Lord's Word, ourselves, and each other better. We have different gifts and different abilities as the Lord has blessed us. Our ministries will be different in many respects.

As we respect those differences, however, and acknowledge a certain relativity to our work as pastors and lay people, there is a point at which the ministry ceases to be relative, and where absolutes take over—not only in creed, but in deed as well. Where that point is, is sometimes hard to determine. But it is there.

To find it in our individual calling will take a lifetime of work. That work must be done and to that end I offer this book.

The publishing arm of a confessional church body such as the Wisconsin Synod is used to producing materials that are safely in the "black" areas of solid exegesis and doctrine. Yet, there is also a place for publishing a book that ventures into the "gray" area, where principle meets application, and whose purpose is to foster discussion on applying principles. My thanks to Northwestern Publishing House for publishing a book that attempts to do both. Special thanks to Rev. Cap Ehlke for his pastoral and professional help in preparing the manuscript for publication.

OVERVIEW

The past did not happen by accident. There were wise men then as there are now. And, whether by design or by instinct, they did things in a good way for their time. Perhaps things went more slowly in the past and people had a better chance of keeping their bearings. A fad was scrutinized over time; the good was taken and the rest was left to die.

Is it just imagination, or are things happening more quickly today? We don't seem to have the time to look long and hard at some new idea, lest we create a backlog of analysis that will never get sorted out. We yearn for a simple filter through which to pass the ideas and methods we are exposed to. We don't want our future to happen by accident.

Can such a filter be found? Some would simply say it's impossible.[1] Using an interesting diagram, however, we can develop a "fulcrum" that will enable us to move methods from the past into the closing decade of the twentieth century.

We intend to show that when we understand the gospel as defined in Scripture and in Lutheran writings, the gospel itself will be both the filter and the fulcrum.

---

[1]Charles Taber, "Contextualization," *Exploring Church Growth,* ed. Wilbert R. Shenk (Grand Rapids: Eerdmans, 1983), p. 122.

The gospel itself will filter out methods that are not appropriate to its spread, and it will provide the fulcrum on which the church can place its lever to move itself through succeeding generations.

Sound complicated? It's really not. Let's take a look at the diagram on this page.

The diagram

The diagram consists of four circles. The two circles on the left represent the Evangelical/Reformed Church.

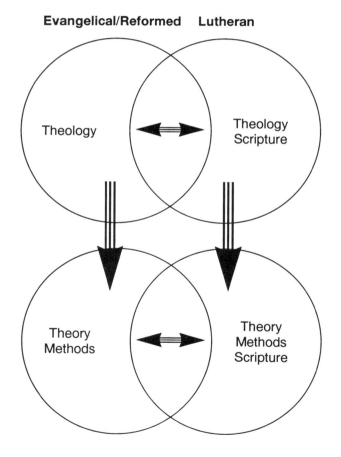

Evangelical/Reformed   Lutheran

Theology

Theology
Scripture

Theory
Methods

Theory
Methods
Scripture

The two circles on the right represent the Lutheran Church. These four circles comprise the four main components that we need to consider if we are to come to grips with Lutheran methodology.

The circles are like the four parts of a simple equation. Three components are known: Both (1) Lutheran and (2) Evangelical/Reformed theology are well documented. An example of (3) Evangelical/Reformed theory and methods is the Church Growth Movement. In this equation the unknown "x" is (4) Lutheran theory and methods.

The top circles intersect. This represents the fact that the theologies of the two churches are not totally distinct, but they share certain teachings in common. The degree of overlap between the two circles is arbitrary. There would be more overlap between some segments of the two churches, and less overlap between others. The same holds true for methods. Some Lutheran churches look more like Evangelical/Reformed churches in their church life, and some Evangelical/Reformed churches look more like historic Lutheran churches.

The arrows that point both ways in the overlapping part of the circles represent the shift that has occurred in Protestant Christianity. The two churches are indeed different. As will be shown in the first part of the book, Luther differed from Calvin and the Swiss Reformers; and modern Lutherans differ from the Evangelical/Reformed. If we are to discover the unknown component of our equation, we will need to understand the basic nature of this difference.

The large arrows pointing downward represent the fact that the way we do things flows out of what we believe. A church acts in the way it does because it accepts certain teachings and has had certain experiences which it tries to reflect in its life and communicate to others.

The bottom circles both contain the words "theory" and "methods." Theory is the underlying set of principles drawn from theology. We try and translate those principles into methods. Methods, however, don't simply refer to special programs, but to our life of faith in general. The word includes everything we do in evangelism, worship, education, social functions, and so on.

I have added the word "Scripture" to both the top and bottom components in Lutheranism for two reasons. First, this book is not simply an academic exercise, analyzing the material in a cool detached way. I am a Lutheran, and I believe that the Lutheran Confessions state the teachings of the Bible. Second, I believe that scriptural theory and methods can only flow from a Lutheran and biblical theology.

While for the sake of our discussion the fourth component will remain an "unknown," I believe that the pastoral and practical aspects of the life of the church are not simply drawn by deduction from the Bible's theology. But the Bible itself gives abundant examples from which we can learn how we should carry out the work of the ministry. I am addressing the fourth component as an unknown so that we can rethink what we are doing in the context of the smorgasbord of methods that has been laid before parish pastors. These methods have come largely through the efforts of an Evangelical/Reformed movement—the Church Growth movement based at Fuller Theological Seminary in Pasadena, California.

Definitions

Two definitions are in order.

"Lutheran" is a term used to describe the theology that is consistent with Martin Luther's teachings and the Confessions of the Lutheran Church as found in the Book of Concord. Not all modern Lutherans acknowledge these two sources. The author is a pastor in a Lutheran Church that strives to base its teachings on the Lutheran Confessions. If the reader is familiar only with the more liberal Evangelical Lutheran Church in America (ELCA), he will have to adjust his definition of Lutheranism while reading this paper.

"Evangelical/Reformed" is a term used to describe that branch of the Reformation Church that finds its roots in the Swiss Reformation, specifically in the theology of John Calvin. This term encompasses a broad range of theologies and denominations. Some of them depart greatly from the teachings of Calvin and parallel the more radical side of the Reformation. There are, however, basic similarities among most Reformed churches today, and in common usage, the term Reformed is still used to distinguish it from Catholicism and Lutheranism.

I will primarily use the term "Reformed" to denote the theology of historic and modern churches that trace their roots back to the Swiss Reformation. I will use the term "Evangelical/Reformed" or simply "Evangelical" when referring to the theology that has been influenced by Arminianism and that is characteristic of churches that call themselves "Evangelical." Into this group falls the majority of those churches that have been influenced by the Church Growth movement.

In Part One we will discuss the differences between Evangelical/Reformed theology and Lutheran theology. This discussion will focus on the nature of the gospel in the Scriptures and in these two churches. Part Two will take us into the realm of Evangelical/Reformed theory and methods. We will discuss theory and methods as they are presented by the Church

Growth School.[2] We will bring the Lutheran understanding of the gospel to bear on Evangelical/Reformed
practice and outline a Lutheran theory, or theology, of
ministry.

---

[2]I recognize that this school does not represent all Evangelical/Reformed
thinking and quite a few authors have disagreed on various points of Church
Growth teaching. But I believe that Church Growth represents the essence of
Reformed methodology and does not depart essentially from what the Evan-
gelical world in general is doing. For some alternate views see Delos Miles,
Church Growth: A Mighty River (Nashville: Broadman Press, 1981), pp. 134-
146, (Baptist); Charles Van Engen, *The Church Growth of the True Church*
(Amsterdam: Rodopi, 1981), (Classic Dutch Reformed) (Note that Van Engen
currently teaches in Fuller's School of World Missions); Shenk, *Exploring
Church Growth,* (Liberal); Ralph Elliot, *Church Growth That Counts* (Valley
Forge: Judson Press, 1982), pp. 53-88, (Liberal? Baptists). Magazine articles
include, J. Randall Peterson, "Church Growth," *Christianity Today* (March
27, 1981), pp. 18-23; J. Eugene Wright, "Church Growth: Ultimate or Penultimate?" *The Christian Ministry* (January 1979), pp. 11-15.

Part One:

THE LUTHERAN AND EVANGELICAL/ REFORMED VIEW OF THE GOSPEL

1.

THE GOSPEL IN SCRIPTURE

The forgiveness of sins plays a different role in Reformed theology than it does in Lutheranism. Both groups speak about forgiveness and many among the Reformed would identify with a Lutheran evangelism presentation. But a shift has taken place in the Reformed camp, leading not to a denial of forgiveness, but to giving it a different place in the overall scheme of their theology. In the process, the meaning of the gospel and justification undergoes a subtle, yet profound, change.

Before we try and come to grips with this shift, I want to spend some time with Scripture on this issue. What exactly is the good news of the gospel? What is justification? What does it mean that a person is converted?

In this first chapter I hope to show that the heart of the gospel is the announcement of forgiveness, that justification is God's declaration of forgiveness and righteousness imputed to us because of Jesus' work for the world, and that the experience of conversion is contrition over the guilt of sin, followed by faith—the acceptance of God's forgiveness.[1] This chapter and the next will be rather sketchy. Their purpose is to present a basic understanding of the terms, so that we have a starting point from which to define the shift we need to be aware of and avoid.

The scriptural meaning of the gospel

The word gospel simply means "good news." It is the good news that the church has been given to preach. Sometimes the term carries the wider meaning of the whole story about Jesus and God's work through him. For example, the story of Mary's anointing Jesus' feet would be told "wherever the gospel is preached throughout the world" (Mark 14:9).[2] Mark begins his book with the words, "the beginning of the gospel about Jesus Christ, the Son of God" (Mark 1:1). In Romans 2:16, Paul includes the message of God's judgment on the world as part of his gospel.

But the gospel also takes a narrower focus. It is "good news" about something specific. What is that something? We could start anywhere in the Bible, but a good place would be the story of Philip and the Ethiopian eunuch. Humanly speaking, the Lord had a limited amount of time to work on the Ethiopian's heart. If we assume that God directed the Ethiopian's choice of what to read that day, we see that God prepared the setting by having

---

[1]Contrition here is part of repentance in the wide sense. It does not refer to a sorrow for sins because they have offended God. Rather, it refers to a terror that a hopeless person feels when confronted by the demands of God's law and the punishment due him for his sins. It prepares for faith not because it leads one to search for God, but because it empties one of any claim on God's favor.

[2]All Scripture references are from the New International Version of the Bible.

4

Philip find him reading Isaiah 53. There Isaiah describes the sufferings and death of Christ—"a sheep led to the slaughter" (Acts 8:32, 33). Beginning at that point, Philip "told him the good news about Jesus" (Acts 8:35). In the context of Isaiah 53, there can be no doubt that the substitutionary work of Jesus by which he paid for the eunuch's sins was foremost in their discussion.

When Peter spoke to Cornelius the centurion, he defined the good news as "peace through Jesus Christ" (Acts 10:36). At the end of his sermon, he stated what sort of peace Christ brought: "All the prophets testify about him that everyone who believes in him receives forgiveness of sins through his name" (Acts 10:43). From these two examples we see that the gospel is primarily a message. It is something that is to be accepted as true, or believed.

The Bible writers continually speak about the gospel as being "facts" that people accept. Peter spoke to the Jerusalem Council and referred to his encounter with Cornelius and how God had "made a choice among you that the Gentiles might hear from my lips the message of the gospel and believe" (Acts 15:7). Paul speaks about his task as "testifying to the gospel of God's grace" (Acts 20:24) and "preaching the gospel of his Son" (Romans 1:9). St. Paul reminded the Ephesians that they were included in Christ when they believed what they heard— "the word of truth, the gospel of your salvation" (Ephesians 1:13). At Colossae faith sprang from the "hope that is stored up for you in heaven" and this hope was what they had "already heard about in the word of truth, the gospel" (Colossians 1:5).

What is the content of the gospel message? In the sermons recorded in the book of Acts, the emphasis is on leading people to realize their guilt and the punishment they deserved for their sins, and then leading them to find peace in Christ's death and resurrection. Peter in

5

his Pentecost sermon did not point out his hearers' alienation from God as evidenced by the personal problems in their lives, but drove them to that realization by telling them that Jesus would return to judge them—Jesus "whom [they] crucified" but who was now "Lord and Christ" (Acts 2:36).

St. Paul preached this same message to the people in Pisidian Antioch. He said, "We tell you the good news: What God promised our fathers he has fulfilled for us, their children, by raising up Jesus" (Acts 13:32,33). What God foretold to the Patriarchs of the Old Testament is the good news that Christ would bring forgiveness of sins to the entire world. For example, Paul says in Galatians 3:8, "The Scripture foresaw that God would justify the Gentiles by faith, and announced the gospel in advance to Abraham: 'All nations will be blessed through you.'"

Paul refers to this point at the end of his sermon in Acts 13 when he says, "Therefore, my brothers, I want you to know that through Jesus the forgiveness of sins is proclaimed to you. Through him everyone who believes is justified from everything you could not be justified from by the law of Moses" (Acts 13:38,39) Granted, not every sermon in Acts states the message of forgiveness so clearly, or uses the term "justify." Nevertheless, all those sermons (Acts 3:12ff; 4:8ff; 17:22ff) were aimed at leading the people to know the guilt of sin, and to base their hope on the message of peace and forgiveness through Christ.

Statements in the Epistles also define the content of the gospel. In Romans 1:17 Paul states, "For in the gospel a righteousness from God is revealed, a righteousness that is by faith." The discussion that follows in 1:18 through 5:21 shows that the righteousness of God that the gospel reveals is God's declaration of our forgiveness through Christ. The gospel is good news against the backdrop of sin and the law (Romans 3:20). It might be added that in this section of Romans, the victory of the Christian over the power of sin is not central to the discussion. Rather, the discussion centers on the guilt of sin and God's wrath against it.

We should note also Paul's statements to the Corinthians in the first two chapters of his first letter. He states that Christ sent him to "preach the gospel—not with words of human wisdom, lest the cross of Christ be emptied of its power" (1 Corinthians 1:17). The ensuing discussion tells us that the cross of Christ was at the center of Paul's understanding of the gospel. The cross is important not because it influences us morally, but because it is "wisdom from God—that is, our righteousness, holiness and redemption" (1 Corinthians 1:30). In the gospel, Christ gives us his righteousness, his holiness, and the announcement that he has redeemed us through his sufferings and death on the cross and his resurrection from the dead.

The gospel, then, is the good news of sin forgiven.

The meaning of justification in Scripture[3]

The English expressions "make righteous" and "justify" are both translations of the Greek verb: *dikaiow*. The

---

[3]The Lutheran reader should understand that this section is a review of some of the basics of our theology. The Evangelical reader is directed to more thorough discussions of this important point in Henry Hamann, "Justification by Faith in Modern Theology" (Th.D. dissertation, Concordia Theological Seminary, Saint Louis, Missouri, 1956.) This is one of the most complete exegetical and theological discussions on the subject available. See also Lorman Peterson, "The Nature of Justification," *Christian Faith and Modern Theology,* ed. Carl F. H. Henry (New York: Channel Press, 1964), pp. 348-370. This is a shorter article and perhaps would serve as a good introduction to the Evangelical on this subject from a Lutheran point of view. An excellent discussion of 2 Corinthians 5:19-21 on this subject is found in John P. Meyer, Ministers of Christ (Milwaukee: Northwestern Publishing House, 1963), pp. 98-119. Siegbert Becker, "Lecture Notes on Romans 1-3,9," transcribed from audio tapes by Rev. Gerhold Lemke is an excellent popular presentation. Note particularly the discussion of Romans 1:17 and chapter three. C. F. W. Walther, *The Proper Distinction Between Law and Gospel* (Saint Louis: Concordia, 1929?), discusses this understanding of justification throughout and applies it to the ministry.

question is whether that term denotes God's act of *giving* a person the gift of righteousness, or whether it means God's act of *making* him righteous. Relating this question to the discussion above, if the gospel is first of all God's message that we can be saved from the domination of sinful actions, the meaning of justification would center on God's power to make us righteous in our lives. On the other hand, if the gospel is the message of forgiveness, justification becomes a declaration of "not guilty" on the sinner.

As we turn to St. Paul for his definition, we'll only consider a few of the main passages. The book of Romans sets the pace for all subsequent use of the word. Paul writes, "I am not ashamed of the gospel, because it is the power of God for the salvation of everyone who believes. . . . For in the gospel a righteousness [*dikaiosune*] from God is revealed, a righteousness that is by faith" (Romans 1:16,17).

What is this righteousness from God? Theologian Siegbert Becker describes it in this way: "The 'righteousness of God' (1:17) is not the righteousness which God has, but the righteousness which God gives me when he justifies me. . . . You dig out this meaning of 'the righteousness of God' by reading the rest of Romans."[4]

The meaning of the "righteousness (or justice) of God" becomes clear as we examine several passages in the first five chapters of Romans. The section following Romans 1:17 continues through 3:20. It contrasts the revelation of God's righteousness with the revelation of his wrath. In 1:18 Paul states that "the wrath of God is being revealed . . . against all the godlessness and wickedness of men." It becomes clear from 2:1 that Paul has

---

[4]Becker, "Notes on Romans 1-3,9." Siegbert Becker was a professor for many years in the Lutheran Church—Missouri Synod and later in the Wisconsin Evangelical Lutheran Synod at Wisconsin Lutheran Seminary, Mequon, Wisconsin.

everyone in mind, and is saying that God's wrath is revealed against all people, for all have substituted idols for the true God. God reveals his wrath against people by letting them go their own way, and becoming engrossed in all sorts of sins, and suffering in themselves the penalty they (we) deserve. In Romans 3:10,11 Paul summarizes, "There is no one righteous, not even one; there is no one who understands, no one who seeks God."

The law is given, "so that every mouth may be silenced and the whole world held accountable to God. Therefore no one will be declared righteous [*dikaiothesetai*] in his sight by observing the law; rather, through the law we become conscious of sin" (Romans 3:19,20).

With this established, Paul returns to the thought he introduced in Romans 1:16,17. He writes in 3:21, "But now a righteousness from God, apart from law, has been made known." This in a nutshell is the "gospel" he introduced earlier. It is a message about another righteousness, one that comes by being revealed to us. Paul had already said that we could not be justified by the law, for the law only makes us conscious of our sin. It is good news that there is another source of righteousness through which we can be just in God's eyes.

It is a "righteousness from God [that] comes through faith in Jesus Christ to all who believe" (Romans 3:22). Paul continues, "for all have sinned and fall short of the glory of God, and are justified freely by his grace through the redemption that came by Christ Jesus" (Romans 3:23,24). Note the parallel: "all have sinned"— "[all] are justified." The natural way of understanding this verse is to maintain the parallel: Just as we are all sinners, so we are all justified, because when Christ died for the sins of the world, he acquired a righteousness that was credited to all people.

It is an objective truth—an objective justification— that depends not on man's acceptance of it, but on

Christ's work. "Faith in his blood" (Romans 3:25) is that which enables a person to benefit from it. Yet, even if I were to refuse to believe that God has justified me, and even if I were to die and go to hell, the failure would have been mine in not using the time of grace God gave me to come to faith.

We can understand this section of Romans only if we accept the reality of God's anger against us because of our sins, and rejoice in Christ's work of gaining a righteousness that God uses as his basis for "justifying" us (or declaring us just). Paul states that because of Christ's work of atonement, God can "be just and the one who justifies those who have faith in Jesus" (Romans 3:26). In other words, God takes sinners and declares them to be just. Nor does he contradict his inherent justice by not punishing sins for which the sinner deserves punishment. The price has been paid; the sinner is righteous in Christ.

In the following chapters of Romans, this idea comes to the fore again and again. Paul gives two examples from the Old Testament of men who were justified in the sense of being given the gift of imputed righteousness. Abraham's faith was "credited to him as righteousness" (Romans 4:3). David considered himself blessed because he was among those "whose transgressions are forgiven, whose sins are covered" (Romans 4:7).

At the end of chapter 4, Paul links the objective fact of justification with the resurrection of Christ. Paul writes, "He was delivered over to death for our sins, and was raised to life for our justification" (Romans 4:25). Here Paul is saying that Christ was put to death because of the sins of humankind, and that he was raised to life because the world had been justified through his taking on himself the punishment of our sins. Henry Hamann writes,

10

Transgression called for punishment, hence the deliverance into death and the cross; but the end of such deliverance into death for sin was that man should be pronounced not-guilty, hence the resurrection of Jesus. The resurrection is the demonstration that all the claims of sin have really been met . . . . The assertion is most emphatically made that justification is there already in the resurrection of Christ. The meaning certainly is not that Christ was raised so that at certain future time when various people have been given a new position through faith God may justify them. Justification was there already when Christ rose. Justification is an objective fact of God's declaring, and the sign of it to men is the resurrection of the Lord Jesus Christ.[5]

In Romans 5, Paul says that we are at peace with God, "since we have been justified through faith" (5:1). Anyone who says that peace comes to us because we have undergone a process of moral renewal is doing injustice to Paul's words, and undermining the peace a Christian ought to have. Paul, in 5:9,10, argues that God in his love came to the world of sinners and justified

---

[5]Hamann, "Justification by Faith," pp. 107,108. In this present book, the entire work of Christ, beginning with his obedience, his sufferings and death, and culminating in his resurrection, are included in the phrase "the work of Christ" and should be understood whenever the idea of forgiveness of sins is spoken about. Although Christ's resurrection means that we will rise, it gives us that assurance because it is the seal that Christ's sacrificial work has been successfully completed. The fact that the resurrected Christ is living in us assures us of his resurrection. But we must always understand that the "Christ who is in us" is there imparting the benefits of the work he has done "for us." See Martin Chemnitz, *Examination of the Council of Trent,* part 1, trans. Fred Kramer (Saint Louis: Concordia, 1971), p. 503. He writes "The most absolute righteousness which the Law demands and requires of us, may be fulfilled not by us but in us, because Christ, who has fulfilled the Law for us, is in us; that is, He dwells in us through faith (Ephesians 3:17)."

11

them. If this is so, is there any doubt that God will accept us as his sons and daughters?

The idea of imputation comes out even more strongly in the second half of chapter 5. Paul argues that because of Adam's sin, death came to every inhabitant of the world. He argues that death came not because of the personal sins of humankind, but because Adam's sin was credited against them. Before the law was given to Moses, he asserts, sin was in existence. But since there was no standard by which to judge sin, people's sins were not credited against them. Yet they still died. Why? Because Adam's sin against the only direct command God had given prior to Moses' time—the command not to eat of the "tree of the knowledge of good and evil"—was credited against his descendants, and brought death on them.

Adam was a type of Christ. Just as Adam's sin was credited to the world, so Christ's righteousness was credited to the world. The idea of imputation is so strongly brought out in 5:12-14 that "justification" in verses 18 and 19 cannot be viewed in any way but a declarative, objective statement. In other words, "the one act of righteousness" that resulted in "justification" that "brings life for all men" was something that was imputed to the world as a whole (Romans 5:18,19).

In Romans 8:33,34, Paul writes, "It is God who justifies. Who is he that condemns?" Just as condemnation is here a forensic act, so justification—the opposite of condemnation—is also a forensic act.

One of the most important Scripture passages for a discussion of the nature of the gospel is 2 Corinthians 5:19-21. Although the term "justification" is not used here, the same idea is set forth under the term "reconciliation." Paul's calling was to be an ambassador of a message. The message was that "God was reconciling the world to himself in Christ, not counting men's sins against them" (2 Corinthians 5:19).[6] This is hardly a message of some moral or societal change God was effecting in the world. Rather, it is an activity that God did through Christ when he offered his Son on the cross for our sins.

Paul concludes this section by saying, "God made him who had no sin to be sin for us, so that in him we might become the righteousness of God" (2 Corinthians 5:21). It was the fact of imputed righteousness, a fact that had universal application, that was Paul's message. To be or remain reconciled to God, which is what Paul urged his hearers, was possible only because God was reconciled to the world already in Christ. Reconciliation is certainly a relational idea. But God's relation to us is based on a forensic act—Christ for us. The gospel message is the announcement that God's relationship with us has changed because of Christ.

The meaning of conversion in Scripture

Lutheran theology is based on a distinct conversion experience, just as Reformed theology is. But these experiences are different. The difference has nothing to do with depth of feeling, or the empirical results of the conversion experience. Rather, the Lutheran conversion comes from faith in the gospel of God's forgiveness, while the Reformed conversion contains elements that relate more to a desire to place oneself under the rule of God's moral law, coupled with a desire to serve God. We will show this in subsequent chapters.

Before we can discuss this more fully, we need to understand how the Bible describes conversion. The mean-

---

[6]On the tense of the Greek verb translated "was reconciling" see J. P. Meyer, *Ministers of Christ* (Milwaukee: Northwestern Publishing House, 1963), pp. 109,110. Meyer argues that the tense does not imply an ongoing activity of bringing people to faith, but rather refers to the objective reconciliation God effected when he sacrificed his Son on the cross.

ing of conversion is directly related to the meaning of the gospel and justification.

Conversion literally means a turning around. But what sort of turning around is it? There are not many conversion accounts in the New Testament, but the several that are there give us a good idea of the nature of conversion as the Bible writers understand it. We will look at them in the order they appear.

Zacchaeus

Luke recounts the story of Zacchaeus, a tax collector who wanted to see Jesus (Luke 19:1-9). Just what Zacchaeus had heard about Jesus, or why he wanted to see him, is not told us. From the discussion that follows, though, we see that Zacchaeus came to faith in Jesus as his Savior from sin. Jesus links Zacchaeus with Abraham and declares, "Today salvation has come to this house, because this man, too, is a son of Abraham. For the Son of Man came to seek and to save what was lost" (Luke 19:9,10).

What he meant by calling Zacchaeus "a son of Abraham" is stated by St. Paul, "And he [Abraham] is also the father of the circumcised who not only are circumcised but who also walk in the footsteps of the faith that our father Abraham had before he was circumcised" (Romans 4:12).

As we have seen, the faith Paul talks about here is faith in God's promise of a Savior, and the gift of righteousness. Zacchaeus was a son of Abraham because he had this faith also.

The criminal on the cross

The criminal on the cross (Luke 23:39-43) at first maligned Jesus, but during the time they spent together on the cross, this man came to faith in Jesus. As in the case of Zacchaeus, I do not believe the text gives us a full picture of what was going on in this man's mind when he was converted. However, we hear him say two things that demonstrate that his conversion came as a result of his coming to know the forgiveness he had in Christ. We hear that he confessed his sins. He said, "We are punished justly, for we are getting what our deeds deserve. But this man has done nothing wrong" (Luke 23:41). He then states his request to Jesus in a very unique way, "Jesus, remember me when you come into your kingdom." The fact that this man used the term kingdom at a time like this—when the one he was praying to was hanging on a cross—tells us that somehow he had come to realize that Jesus was no ordinary king. He may have heard the crowds yelling hosanna to the Son of David. But unlike the crowds who may have mistaken Christ's entry into Jerusalem as a bid for secular power, this man was facing Jesus who was about to die. Yet in that context he used the word "kingdom." Based on what we will see in the next chapter, I believe the only conclusion we can come to is that the thief was confessing that Christ's kingdom was established on the basis of his death, a death that took away the sins of the world—including his.

Nicodemus

Jesus' discussion with Nicodemus clearly points out how conversion is contrition and faith in God's forgiveness. After talking about the necessity of being born a second time, "of water and the Spirit" (John 3:5), Jesus describes the working of the Spirit, "The wind blows wherever it pleases. You hear its sound, but you cannot tell where it comes from or where it is going. So it is with everyone born of the Spirit" (John 3:8). This might be understood as describing a general conversion to God or it might describe a decision to serve Christ as Lord. But in the following discussion, Jesus centers the work

15

of the Spirit on his leading people to know that Jesus has died for their sins.

The well known statements in verses 15 and 16 point to the cross and Christ's substitutionary death on it. To "believe" in Christ is to know one's sin and to believe in the fact that on the cross Christ has died for that sin. Faith certainly is shown by its fruits (John 3:19-21), but it is belief in Christ as the Savior from sin that delivers from death and hell.

We will have occasion to discuss the conversion of the woman at the well in Samaria (John 4) in a later section. Here we will simply note that Jesus pointed out her sins also, and that she too came to faith in him when he told her that he was the Christ.

The Ethiopian eunuch

The eunuch from Ethiopia was a believer in the God of the Old Testament (Acts 8:26-40). His conversion was like that of many at the time of Christ and shortly afterward. He came to faith in Jesus as the Messiah he had been awaiting.

The Lord told Philip to approach the Eunuch. If we agree that the Lord chose the time for the meeting, we gain an insight into what he considers to be the "center" of conversion. The Eunuch was reading Isaiah 53. Specifically, he was reading about the prophecy of Christ's crucifixion as the Lamb of God (Acts 8:32,33). It was the Eunuch's questions about this section on the vicarious work of Jesus that gave Philip the opportunity to talk about Christ.

St. Paul

St. Paul's conversion is often used as an example of a dramatic conversion of a man who was looking for something better. There is no doubt that Paul's conversion was dramatic, but it was dramatic not because it was the end of a long "search" by Paul for something better in his life. Rather, because Paul was such an open antagonist of the church, God saw fit to use something dramatic to bring him to faith.

Paul needed such an experience if he was to witness in the role God called him to fill. Paul's conversion centered on his coming to know his sins, and realizing that the one whom he was persecuting was his Savior.

All of Paul's writings reflect this fact. For example, in Philippians 3:7ff he states that his hope lay not in his works, but in Christ's righteousness. To "know Christ" and to "gain Christ" was not a general infusion of power, but for Paul it meant to be "found in him, not having a righteousness of my own that comes from the law, but that which is through faith in Christ—the righteousness that comes from God and is by faith" (Philippians 3:9). We should also note that "the power of his [Christ's] resurrection" about which Paul speaks in Philippians 3:10 is based on his knowing the righteousness of Christ that God had given him as a gift, through faith.

Summary

This brief chapter was not meant to provide an exhaustive doctrinal treatment of these subjects, but rather to form a basic foundation for the points made later in this book. The gospel and justification refer to the forgiveness of sins that Jesus has won for us on the cross. Conversion is turning to God as a consequence of realizing the personal guilt of one's sins, and believing that Jesus has forgiven that guilt. Jesus' victory over the guilt of sin must remain at the center of our thinking on these topics.

2.

THE GOSPEL OF THE KINGDOM

In the last chapter we asked questions. The "gospel"—good news about what? "Conversion"—what kind of change is it? "Justification"—is it a change or a verdict? In this chapter we want to ask some questions about the "kingdom of God." A kingdom implies a king and the activity of ruling. But how does Christ rule? And what is the relationship between him and his subjects?

The kingdom of God is one of the most important themes in the Bible. In fact, one might call it the skeleton around which most of the talk of salvation in both the Old and New Testaments is formed.

The goal of this chapter will be to show that the kingdom of God is nothing other than God's reigning through his message of justification and reconciliation. The teaching of the kingdom of God in Scripture does not begin with or center on a change that takes place in the subjects, although the subjects cannot but change. The kingdom of God centers on the cross of Christ, and being a member of that kingdom means living under God in peace because our sins are forgiven.

The gospel of the kingdom in the Old Testament

Adam and Eve

The kingdom of God must be seen in relation to creation and the fall into sin recorded in Genesis 1-3. Although the term kingdom is not used in those chapters, the basic elements necessary for understanding the kingdom are. In a sense, already at creation God had established a kingdom. It was a perfect world where man could serve God in holiness and righteousness. It was a place where man was reigning along with God, and the entire creation was subject to them. It was a place where God would personally commune with Adam and Eve and bestow his blessings on them.

Tragically, this "kingdom" did not last very long. Satan took the one command God had given Adam and Eve—a command that established the fact that ultimate authority belonged to God alone—and used it to lead Adam and Eve into rebellion against God. This destroyed the kingdom. It's not that God had lost his power. But man lost the blessing of being in harmony with God, living peacefully with him, and enjoying the benefits of God's unlimited power.

One might say that the root of man's separation from God and loss of the kingdom lay in the guilt of his sin rather than in the consequences of his sin. Because man had sinned, his attitude toward God had changed. His heart had been filled with nothing but good, but now it became a heart where there was nothing but hostility toward God (Romans 8:7,8). Where there is sin, there can only be a feeling of terror and enmity in God's presence. Adam and Eve knew God was still King, and that thought terrified them because they knew they were not part of his kingdom.

In this setting, God came looking for man. The Lord came looking for man not merely with a general love and an invitation to seek God. Nor did God come with the promise that he would erase the physical affects of Adam and Eve's sin. The physical curses had not even been pronounced when God came searching for man. When he confronted Adam and Eve he found only hostility—"the woman *you* gave to me." He found only selfishness and denial—"the *woman* you gave to me." He found two people who were afraid of him. But he gave them a promise and it was this promise that assured them that they could stand before God and worship him again.

In Genesis 3:14,15 we have an outline of the reestablishment of the kingdom of God for Adam and Eve. In verse 14 God condemned the serpent to "eat dust all the days of your life." What a wonderful message for Adam and Eve! The one who had tempted them and in whose kingdom they now lived would "eat dust." Isaiah certainly had this passage in mind when he described God's kingdom which the Messiah would establish like this: "The wolf and lamb will feed together, and the lion will eat straw like the ox, but dust will be the serpent's food" (Isaiah 65:25).

Verse 15 begins with more good news. At the time these words were spoken, Adam and Eve were in a state of hostility toward God. You could say they were at enmity with God and at peace with Satan. But God told Satan in their hearing, "And I will put enmity between you and the woman, and between your offspring and hers." While this would cause the woman and her offspring persecution at the hands of Satan and his offspring, this was still music to their ears. For being "at enmity" with Satan meant that they were now at peace with God.

20

Why could they hope for this peace? The answer is given in the next phrase, "He will crush your head, and you will strike his heel." One of the offspring of the woman would crush Satan's head. This refers to the Promised One who would later be called the Messiah, the Anointed of God. To translate this into kingdom terms: the crushing of Satan's head was the foundation of God's kingdom in the scriptural sense. It was the reason his kingdom could be established. Now Adam, Eve, and all people could hope to live under God and receive his blessings here on earth and into eternity.

It was only after the promise was given that God sent curses on the human race. Both physical burdens and the curse of death are major sources of suffering that human beings should expect on this earth.

In one sense, the physical curses God placed on the world were signs of his separation from mankind, but in another sense they were not. Even these curses were part of God's gracious rule on behalf of his people. The reason God sent them was so that man would number his days and apply his heart to wisdom (Psalm 90:12). Through these difficulties, God was leading people to release their naturally tight grasp on this world and look forward to the restoration of all things at the end of time. The fact that his creation "was subjected to frustration" (Romans 8:20), does not mean that God's kingdom is not in effect at the present time. It is.

In all things God is working for the good of his people. This doesn't mean we should take a grim, fatalistic attitude about God's dealing with us, for certainly God can alleviate our sufferings as he did in the days following the Flood. (See Genesis 5:29.) And, in love, we will want to help alleviate the suffering of others as much as we can. Yet we should always remember that the curse will remain until God brings this age to an end. Jesus remains in control and the kingdom of God is still in full force even during the time the curse is in effect.

The Patriarchs: Abraham and Jacob

In Genesis 12, we see God blessing Abraham and saying that he would be a blessing to all nations. Sometimes it is here, instead of in Genesis 3, that a serious discussion of God's blessing to mankind begins.[1] Some theologians assert that Abraham was "blessed to be a blessing." This is true; but it's necessary to keep in mind the promise given in Genesis 3, and interpret this blessing specifically as referring to Abraham's ancestorship of the Savior. Otherwise, the interpretation of Abraham's blessing becomes too general.

With Genesis 3 in mind, we realize God was telling Abraham that he had been chosen to be the father of the Savior. His faith in this promise "was credited to him as righteousness," not because he had a general faith in God whom he was obeying but because he believed that God's promise to him was simply a restatement of the promise that someone would crush the head of the serpent. His faith had a very specific object. Abraham knew he was blessed by having the Savior born from his descendants, and that through the Savior people from all nations would come under God's reign of grace and forgiveness.

Kingdom terminology actually begins in Genesis 49. There Abraham's grandson Jacob blessed his son Judah and said, "The scepter will not depart from Judah, nor the ruler's staff from between his feet, until he comes to whom it belongs and the obedience of the nations is his" (Genesis 49:10).

---

[1]This is evident in the Bethel Bible Series where the promise of a Savior in Genesis 3 is hardly emphasized. Also, in the three sessions at Fuller, I never heard the promise of Genesis 3 referred to, although the promise in Genesis 12 was referred to a number of times.

David and the Kingdom of Israel after him

David, the son of Jesse, was the first great king of Israel. He was also a type of Christ, the King. Throughout the Old Testament God promised to place someone on David's throne whose kingdom would last forever (for example, 2 Samuel 7:11-16).

After David's death, there were troublesome times for his kingdom. The sinful lusts of the people turned their eyes from God to idols. All during the wretched years of the divided kingdom, God sent prophets to warn the people to repent, but they refused.

Yet throughout those long and wearisome chapters of the Bible where gloom and destruction are prophesied, the vision of the future kingdom of God remained alive, sometimes appearing in the biblical text with no warning. In one verse a prophet might be talking about how God would punish the people for their sins and in the next he is speaking about God's gracious rule in which he will change the hearts of his people, restore their fortunes, and, in short, establish for them a kingdom in which he will be their God. What a change from what the prophets saw going on around them!

How would God establish this kingdom? This is the key question. Would it come about through God's powerful intervention in the history of the world—through a confrontation of power by which God would convince people once and for all that he was real and thereby change their hearts and lead them into his service? No. The establishment of the kingdom hinged on the Messiah's completion of his work of crushing the serpent's head. In other words, the prophets made it clear that God would be King when Jesus completed his work of keeping the law in our place, taking our sins on himself on the cross, and rising again as the Victor.

To trace this idea throughout the Old Testament is beyond the scope of this book. One section, though, deserves note. In my opinion, from the standpoint of understanding the establishment of God's kingdom, Isaiah 53 is the major chapter in the Old Testament.

This magnificent chapter falls into the second part of Isaiah, the section of Isaiah's prophecy that foresees the time when God would allow Israel to return from the Babylonian captivity. God's act of enabling Israel to return to Palestine is a picture of the establishment of his kingdom under Christ. The second section of the book of Isaiah also looks ahead to the new heaven and new earth that God will establish at the end of time.

The section is thirty-seven chapters long. The middle chapter, the one on which everything hinges, is chapter 53.[2] There Isaiah tells about the foundation of the kingdom—the suffering of the Lord's servant. Because the servant suffered, the Lord would raise him up and exalt him. "Therefore I will give him a portion among the great, and he will divide the spoils with the strong, because he poured out his life unto death, and was numbered with the transgressors" (Isaiah 53:12). We find here an important point we will refer to again in chapter 5: Christ is our King because he was first our Priest who gave himself as our sacrifice. In his commentary on Isaiah II, August Pieper writes:

> The idea of a suffering Servant of the Lord, who through suffering rises to superhuman glory, is indicated at the very beginning of the Old Testament (Gen. 3:15), and now and then in later passages (Num. 21); it was symbolized by the sacrificial offerings, and typified in David (Ps. 8, 16, 22, etc.). But it was not until Isaiah began to proph-

---

[2]I realize that English chapter divisions prove nothing. However, the section beginning at 52:13 is also at the middle of Isaiah from the standpoint of content and outline. See August Pieper, *Isaiah II,* trans. Erwin Kowalke (Milwaukee: Northwestern Publishing House, 1979), p. 3.

esy that this idea was directly and thoroughly developed.[3]

The transition period: Mary and Zechariah

What did the Jewish people expect when they envisioned their promised kingdom? Probably most expected an outward kingdom in which God would improve the condition of the world under the leadership of the Jews. Others understood the true nature of Christ's kingdom. Two examples are Mary and Zechariah. These two are of interest, for they expressed in Old Testament terms their hope that was soon to be fulfilled in Christ.

Mary sang a song in which she rejoiced that the kingdom was now going to be established. She said,

> He has performed mighty deeds with his arm; he has scattered those who are proud in their inmost thoughts. He has brought down rulers from their thrones but has lifted up the humble. . . . He has helped his servant Israel, remembering to be merciful to Abraham and his descendants forever, even as he said to our fathers. (Luke 1:51-55)

Zechariah is even more explicit. Note that when he spoke he was filled with the Holy Spirit. His words were not wishful thinking, but a revelation of what the Savior would do. He would redeem his people (Luke 1:68), give us "salvation from our enemies" (1:71), and enable us "to serve him without fear" (1:74). His words addressed to his son John bear repeating,

> And you, my child, will be called a prophet of the Most High; for you will go on before the Lord to prepare the way for him, to give his people the

---

[3]Pieper, *Isaiah II*, p. 458.

knowledge of salvation through the forgiveness of their sins, . . . to guide our feet into the path of peace. (Luke 1:76-79)

Salvation would not simply bring with it the forgiveness of sins, but salvation would come through the forgiveness of sins. Christ's obedient life, sacrificial death, and victorious resurrection, had won forgiveness, and given us the victory over the guilt of sin, the specter of death, and the might of the devil.

The kingdom of God in the New Testament

A complete description of the kingdom of God as presented in the New Testament is impossible at this point. We will merely summarize the main points and look at a collage of passages describing the nature of the kingdom.

The kingdom of God is God's reign over all things, based on the work of Jesus his Son. It is, first of all, a reign of grace. This means that God comes to sinners with the message of his Son's atoning work on the cross. Those who believe the message come to possess the hope it brings and grow in holy living just as they are holy through Christ's forgiveness. By definition, this reign includes a "flip side." Salvation means judgment on sin, death, and Satan. It includes the eradication of all evil, including the destruction of God's enemies at the end of time.

When John the Baptist announced that the kingdom of God was near, he told the people to repent and believe the good news. By telling them to repent, John was saying that people should face the fact that the kingdom included their destruction if they stood against God and did not submit to his gift of righteousness. (See Romans 10:3.) He encouraged the people to repent and believe the good news that God's reign was now being established in Christ, the "Lamb of God who takes away the sin of the world" (John 1:29). The fruits of repentance were to follow. But it was the kingdom that produced the fruits, not the fruits that produced the kingdom.

When Jesus performed the signs of the kingdom, he was doing just that—giving signs of the victory he had won over the forces of evil, signs that pointed to the time when he would bring total relief to God's people and total destruction to his enemies. When Jesus preached, he pointed people to himself, not in a general sort of way as teacher, exemplar, or even as the sovereign God. He pointed them to himself as the one whose death would establish God's kingdom.

To Jesus, as to John, repentance was the key to entering God's kingdom. Again, repentance does not first of all mean that a person turns from sin, but that a person has a contrite heart and knows himself to be a sinner. Such a person comes with empty hands and joins with the repentant thief on the cross in saying, "Lord, remember me when you come into your kingdom," and then with joy hears Jesus' reply, "Today . . . ." Jesus tells us that sinners were entering this kingdom ahead of the righteous, for sinners gladly accepted God's mercy (Matthew 21:31).

The kingdom rests on the fact that Satan has been judged. Revelation 12:10 speaks about the establishment of the kingdom: "Now have come the salvation and the power and the kingdom of our God, and the authority of his Christ." On what basis had it been established? "For the accuser of our brothers, who accuses them before our God day and night, has been hurled down. They overcame him by the blood of the Lamb and by the word of their testimony" (12:10,11).

Two things go together to establish the kingdom. Objectively, it was established when Jesus died for the sins of the world. Shortly before his crucifixion he said, "Now is the time for judgment on this world; now the prince of this world will be driven out" (John 12:31). Subjectively, it is established through the testimony of God's people who bear witness to this truth. When Jesus sent the seventy out to preach, he saw Satan, the accuser, fall like lightning from heaven (Luke 10:18).

The kingdom of God—that is, God's activity through the gospel—establishes the church, "and the gates of hell shall not overcome it," (Matthew 16:18—KJV). Jesus is the one about whom Paul says, "God placed all things under his feet and appointed him to be head over everything for the church" (Ephesians 1:22).

Faith erases any dispute about this, for "God left nothing that is not subject to him. Yet at present we do not see everything subject to him" (Hebrews 2:8). By faith the church accepts this as true. By faith we know that Christ's triumphal march has already taken place, for "having disarmed the powers and authorities, he made a public spectacle of them, triumphing over them by the cross" (Colossians 2:15). We rest secure, for "God placed all things under his feet and appointed him to be head over everything for the church" (Ephesians 1:22). We know that the powers of this world will never harm us, for our Lord "gave himself for our sins to rescue us from the present evil age" (Galatians 1:4).

When the Christian considers his relation to the devil and his power, he knows there is no see-saw power struggle. Christ has already won the total victory over Satan. The only thing Satan can do is to lead a Christian to resist or reject God's mercy and so lead him to forfeit the kingdom. Consequently, a Christian wars against Satan, not with his morals (although they are important), but with the weapons of the gospel which Paul enumerates in Ephesians 6. It is the preaching of the kingdom based on Christ's victory on the cross that is God's power for conversion (1 Corinthians 2:1-5; 4:18-20).

God's kingdom can be resisted. Because the kingdom is God's rule through the gospel message of God's forgiveness for the sinner, the power of the kingdom is a power that many will reject. The disciples had to be prepared for that. They had to know that they were vulnerable to the world's anger and "must go through many hardships to enter the kingdom of God" (Acts 14:22).

The parables of Jesus instruct disciples of all times what the kingdom of God is like. They understand the "secrets of the kingdom of heaven" (Matthew 13:11) The King will forgive the great debt of his servants, but there will be judgment for those whose lack of forgiving others betrays their own unrepentant heart (Matthew 18:22). It is a wonderful rule that many find and treasure (Matthew 13:44,45). They even "pluck out an offending eye" or "cut off an offending foot" to keep from losing the kingdom (Mark 9:45-47). The gospel and God's rule will permeate the world (Matthew 13:31-33), for the "forceful" will let nothing stop them from entering this kingdom (Matthew 11:12). But some will get caught up in the kingdom of this world with its power and allurements, and will give up God's rule (Matthew 13:18,19).

Finally, the righteous will "shine like the sun in the kingdom of their Father" (Matthew 13:43). The rule of God in this present age will be replaced by the rule of God in a new heaven and new earth. God's grace will be the same, but the sin and sufferings that are part of this present world will be removed.

Christ is ruling now, but everything is not yet restored to the perfection it had in the beginning (Acts 3:21). In many places, the New Testament refers to the kingdom as something in the future. When we understand the kingdom to be God's rule in grace, references to the future do not conflict with Jesus' referring to the kingdom as a present reality. The grace and the judgment that are now operative in view of Christ's victory on the cross, will continue when this age ends. His enemies will be consigned to hell and his own will inherit eternal life (Matthew 25:34).

The believer understands the nature of repentance and faith. As a member of the church he or she can use the keys of the kingdom to give forgiveness to a penitent sinner and so open God's kingdom to that person. On the other hand, God's people can tell the unrepentant that because of his impenitence, God's rule of grace is not his (Matthew 16:19). Since the believer has humbled himself like a child and so entered the kingdom, (Matthew 18:1,3,4), he, in humility, can use these "keys" as the Lord wishes. Such is the work of the church.

The church must preach the law that condemns men's sins and speak the gospel that says God has condemned sin in Christ. Only this message will open people to God's kingdom of grace. We become members of the kingdom through forgiveness, and Christ's victory on the cross is the foundation of God's love for us and the basis of his right to condemn his enemies. Consequently, only the message of the cross will determine the true spread of the kingdom and the growth of the church.

Conclusion

In each area we have studied, the work of Christ in bringing about forgiveness plays the central role. The gospel is the message of God's forgiveness. The gospel is justification—both as the declaration of forgiveness for all and as the personal cleansing from the guilt of sin that a person receives by faith in Christ. Conversion is being turned from Satan to God. This can only happen when we come to know that we deserve to be condemned for our sin, but that Christ was condemned in our place.

The kingdom of God is based on Christ's forgiveness and it grows as that message is preached and believed. God rules over all the forces of evil, both spiritual and physical, and will destroy them on the last day. He rules over us because he has enabled us by faith to die with Christ and rise with him free from the guilt of our sins. In this way he leads us to love and serve him. This understanding will serve as our foundation as we evaluate the methodologies of others and seek to establish our own.

3.

TWO DIFFERENT THEOLOGICAL SYSTEMS

The environmentalist John Muir was famous for his statement, "Everything in the universe is connected to everything else." The same can be said about theology. The Bible is a unit. It is not simply a collection of teachings. Everything the Lord teaches us in his Word is joined with everything else, and all the interrelated teachings form a unit.

We might also say the same about theological systems. Each theological system in the world of Christianity is made up of interrelated teachings that together form a unit and lead in a general direction. This applies to Roman Catholic teaching, Lutheran teaching, and Reformed teaching. While there may be divergences of individual doctrines within these general groups, it can be shown that they all follow a basic controlling principle.

That principle gives a distinctive nature to each theological system as a whole and colors the understanding that each system has of its separate teachings.

Both the Reformed and Lutheran elements of the Reformation fought against the Roman Catholic Church. Their common opponent has led many to assume that Reformed teaching and Lutheran teaching are virtually identical, different only in various externals and minor points of doctrine. In today's world, where churches often do not hold the distinctive beliefs that their historical name would seem to attach to them, such a conclusion, while not correct, is understandable.

Yet, in fact, there is a basic difference between the Lutheran Church and the Reformed Church. This difference has to do with what each church considers to be the "center" of Christianity. The difference lies not in peripheral matters, but in the very understanding of the nature of the gospel.

The difference is ...

I hope the discussion of theological differences in the next chapters will result in our coming to a very basic theological understanding. My purpose is not to arrive at a systematic understanding of the theologies. Rather, I hope to arrive at a grass roots understanding of the different theological systems as they act on people in their day-to-day existence, determining their spiritual frame of reference, setting their spiritual goals, and forming their methods of outreach and ministry. If we're going to deal with methods that relate to people who are either first hearing the Word, or who are to be nurtured in it, we cannot work on the airy heights of the classroom. We need to arrive at a point where everyone can relate.

Lutheran theology correctly views man's main problem to be the guilt of his sin; the gospel is nothing other than that in Christ, God has justified the world. Reformed theology is skewed in the direction of making the goal of Christianity the *remaking* of people into more moral individuals.

The differences are not clear cut at denominational borders. Evangelical/Reformed churches contain some elements that I will ascribe to Lutherans. And often Lutheran churches practice their faith in a way more like we might expect from the Reformed. The more purely Lutheran one becomes, however, the more his or her objectives coincide with those I have described above as scriptural. The more consistently one practices the tenets of Reformed theology, the more he or she drifts into an emphasis on bare morality.

The difference is not . . .

It is also important to note what the distinction between Lutheranism and Reformed theology is *not* about.

First, it is not about having a relationship with God. Both theologies are concerned with that. The Lutheran church sees the relation with God as established by God through the vicarious atonement of his Son Jesus on the cross and through his resurrection from the dead. When a person believes this fact, his relation with God is established by faith. Reformed theology views the relation as being established through union with Christ. Such a relation comes through a person's opening himself to God through a decision to turn from his sin, thus preparing the way for God to come and live with him, and impart his blessings.

Second, the distinction is not about the importance of good works. Both theologies consider good works to be important; "cheap grace" is an abomination to both. Lutheran theology, though, views God's grace as something that cost Jesus dearly and which, in one sense, costs a person nothing, yet, in another sense, costs him his entire life. Reformed theology might agree with that statement, but will emphasize more the moral aspects of Christianity, stating that union with Christ must be proven by a certain degree of moral activity.

The reader should note that this book will not be a forum for me to defend all the accusations a Reformed person might have against the Lutheran church, and against the many abuses of God's grace that have appeared in that church in the past or present. This work simply treats the one basic distinction between the Lutheran and Reformed church—their understanding of the gospel.

Third, the distinction is not necessarily about who is a Christian and who is not. There are two spirits working in the world—the Holy Spirit and the spirit of the devil. Both can effect a conversion experience. Both strive to shape the nature of a person's religious life. Conversion and spiritual life that comes from the Spirit of God is true Christianity. That which comes from the other spirit is fake and will lead to eternal death. Both of these spirits can and do reside side by side in every Christian. That is the nature of the Christian—old sinful nature in tune with Satan, and a new being created by the Holy Spirit, residing in the same person. As long as the Spirit of Christ is dwelling in someone, he or she is a Christian even though the other spirit may be present in one degree or another.

My contention is that within the Evangelical/Reformed body of teachings and experience, there lurks a false spirit that in its true form can do nothing but lead a person away from Christ. The spiritual framework I am describing as Lutheran in its pure form comes from the Holy Spirit and can do nothing but lead a person to Christ. Regarding the members of the Evangelical/Reformed churches, it is a happy inconsistency that allows the truth they teach to lead them to Christ *in spite of* the pervasive presence of that other spirit. Regarding

35

members of the Lutheran churches, it is possible for them to follow the ways of the other spirit, even while they live in an environment where the Word and sacraments should lead them straight to Christ.

The false spirit must not be taken lightly. If it is allowed to enter into a church's teachings and practice, it can only harm the cause of faith. I will not be able to make this statement every time I refer to the Evangelical/Reformed denominations, so I wish to emphasize early on that this book is aimed primarily at the false spirit we must guard against. It is not aimed at every teaching of the Evangelical/Reformed churches.

With these basic definitions and qualifications in mind, we are ready to proceed. In the next three chapters we will discuss the difference as it applies to justification, the kingdom of God, and conversion. These subjects do not exhaust the possible areas where the basic distinction between Lutheranism and Reformed theology expresses itself. But they help us understand that difference, especially as it relates to how we establish evangelism programs and carry out the work of the ministry.

4.

THE GOSPEL—
LUTHERAN AND REFORMED

Martin Luther's understanding
of the gospel in general

It is not difficult to discover what Luther understood the gospel to be. He spent his entire life defending his conclusion that the gospel is God's message that through Christ the sinner has been forgiven all his sins.

To Luther, the message of the gospel was the good news that Christ had done something for him. It was an objective fact. For Luther, faith was his troubled heart accepting the fact that when Christ died on the cross, he suffered for his sins also. The object of faith was all-important. The cross of Christ and the work he did on that cross are what the sinner believes in. And by believing in that he is saved.

All the words the Bible uses to describe the good news took on a completely objective meaning for Luther. This doesn't mean there was no subjective side to his faith. There certainly was. No one who has read Luther would deny that he was a man of intense trust and piety; and he demonstrated this in the many sufferings he was called on to endure. Nor does this mean that Luther did not experience the gospel. Luther's experience was so intense that it carried him through the difficult work God called him to do.

To Luther, the objective nature of the gospel and the matter of experience were never opposites. It was just that Luther's personal experience was based on a totally objective fact.

Luther's understanding of justification

Justification by faith alone was the theme of the Lutheran Reformation. Robin Leaver writes, "From the time of this experience—whenever it was—the doctrine of justification by faith alone became his controlling principle."[1]

For Luther, justification began as an objective fact. In other words, the basis for his hope was not that Christ justified Martin Luther by faith, but that God justified the entire world before anyone actually received the benefit of Christ's work by faith. In discussing the Fifth Petition of the Lord's Prayer in the Large Catechism he says,

> This is why there is great need here again to pray and cry: Dear Father, forgive us our trespasses. Not that He does not forgive sin even without and before our prayer; for He has given us the gospel, in which there is nothing but forgiveness, even before we prayed for it or ever

---

[1]Robin A. Leaver, *Luther on Justification* (Saint Louis: Concordia, 1975), p. 13.

thought about it. What we are concerned about in this petition is that we may recognize and accept this forgiveness.[2]

This is not universalism as that term is understood today. Luther wrote, "Christ did indeed suffer for the whole world; but how many are there who believe and cherish this fact? Therefore, although the work of redemption itself has been accomplished, it still cannot help and benefit a man unless he believes it."[3]

Luther's entire theology centered in the teaching of the gospel of God's justification of the world. Faith lays hold of the fact of Christ's message of forgiveness: "Christ came for my sake, in order to free me from the Law, not only from the guilt of sin but also from the power of the Law. If you are able to say yes to this, you have what is called faith."[4]

Even when Luther speaks of Christ being "in us" he has in mind the work that Christ did "for us." For Luther, when Christ comes to live within us, it is to lead us to faith in what he has done for us. He wrote,

Faith justifies because it apprehends and possesses this Treasure, to wit, the present Christ. . . . Therefore Christ, apprehended by faith and dwelling in the heart, is Christian righteousness, for the sake of which God considers (reputat) us just and gives us eternal life. Here there certainly is no work of the Law, no love, but a righteousness different by far and a kind of new world, outside and above the Law.[5]

---

[2]Ewald Plass, ed., *What Luther Says,* vol. 2 (Saint Louis: Concordia, 1959), p. 705.

[3]Ibid., pp. 705,706.

[4]Plass,*What Luther Says,* vol. 1, p. 466.

[5]Plass, *What Luther Says,* vol. 2, p. 708.

Every other term the Scriptures use to discuss the gospel derives its meaning from the teaching of justification. The atonement of Christ becomes the cornerstone of Christianity, for the atonement of Christ is the object of faith.[6] Grace is primarily the forgiveness of sin. Luther wrote, "For Paul teaches a difference between grace, on the one hand, and gifts, on the other. Grace signifies that favor with which God receives us, forgiving our sins and justifying us freely (*gratis*) through Christ. Do not consider it a quality (in man), as the sophists dream it is."[7]

Sanctification always flows from justification. In fact, a person cannot begin to lead a life in service to God unless he knows that his sins have been completely forgiven. Only when justification is viewed as the non-imputation of sin, can any real growth in living as a Christian result:

> He who is justified performs good works; for this is the meaning of Scripture: Justification precedes good works, and works are performed by those who are justified. . . . The works of faith do not make faith, but faith does the works of faith. In like manner the works of grace do not make grace; but grace does the works of grace.[8]

The teaching of justification is also at the heart of the sacraments. In the Catholic Church, the sacraments were means of grace, but in the sense of imparting a quality to those who partook of them. But to Luther, the Sacraments were means of grace because they proclaimed and gave the forgiveness of sins. Luther was not

---

[6]Ibid., p. 709.
[7]Ibid., p. 603.
[8]Ibid., p. 721.

concerned about the sacraments as means of renewal; rather he was concerned about them because he wanted the assurance of God's forgiveness.

Martin Luther wanted nothing other than the assurance of a gracious God. The teaching of justification as the forgiveness of sins answered this need. It was this that Luther saw as the main teaching of the Bible. This teaching was at the center of Lutheranism.

John Calvin and the gospel

In general, the Reformed Churches today can trace their roots back to the branch of the Reformation begun by John Calvin. Calvin was the man who gave a theological framework to the Swiss Reformation.

Is there a difference between the German and Swiss Reformation in the way they understand the gospel? Many would answer no. They would say there is virtually no difference.[9] Many authors, however, do acknowledge that there is indeed a basic difference between the two Reformers.

The first group appeals to Calvin's many statements in which he sounds much like Luther. Without a doubt, many statements from Calvin's writings clearly explain the vicarious atonement of Christ for the sins of the world, and treat justification as a declaration of righteousness in the same way as Luther did. For example, commenting on Isaiah 53:5 Calvin wrote, "Christ was the price of 'our chastisement,' that is, of the chastisement which was due to us. Thus the wrath of God, which had been justly kindled against us, was appeased;

---

[9]For an extended discussion of this point see Hermann Sasse, *Here We Stand,* trans. Theodore Tappert (Saint Louis: Concordia, 1966). Sasse lived in the first part of the twentieth century in Germany at the time of the proposed Lutheran and Reformed merger. His book contains his refutation of various views of the Reformation that tended to downplay the differences between the two churches.

and through the Mediator we have obtained 'peace,' by which we are reconciled.[10]

Even Calvin's doctrine of the election of some to damnation is not as predominant in his works as we are sometimes led to believe. Calvin approaches the universal view of justification that we find in Luther. Again, in his commentary on Isaiah we read, "We ought to draw from this a universal doctrine, namely, that we are reconciled to God by free grace, because Christ hath paid the price of 'our peace.'"[11] He also writes, "Let everyone, therefore, draw consolation from this passage . . . for these words are spoken to all in general, and to individuals in particular."[12] There is no doubt that the gospel as Luther understood it, can be found in various places in Calvin's works. A quick review of the section on justification in the *Institutes* of Calvin shows that his exegesis of such passages as Isaiah 53:5 has carried over into his dogmatics.[13] For example, he says,

> Justified by faith is he who, excluded from the righteousness of works, grasps the righteousness of Christ through faith, and clothed in it, appears in God's sight not as a sinner but as a righteous man.
>
> Therefore, we explain justification simply as the acceptance with which God receives us into his favor as righteous men. And we say that it consists in the remission of sins and the imputation of Christ's righteousness.[14]

---

[10]John Calvin, *Commentary on the Book of the Prophet Isaiah,* trans. William Pringle (Grand Rapids: Eerdmans, 1948), p. 116.

[11]Ibid.

[12]Ibid., p. 117.

[13]John Calvin, *Institutes of the Christian Religion in Two Volumes,* ed. John McNeill (Philadelphia: Westminster, 1960), pp. 725ff.

[14]Ibid., pp. 726,727.

Does this make their understanding of the gospel identical? Not really. First, there are *specific teachings* in Calvin's theology that undermine the gospel. A thorough discussion of Calvin's theology from a dogmatical standpoint is beyond the scope of this book. Ample discussion of these points can be found in various conservative Lutheran dogmatics books.[15] Second, however, it is the *emphasis* Calvin placed on various teachings, the order in which he presented his material, and the nature of his church reforms that shows that we are dealing with a theology (and, to some extent, a spirit) different from Luther's.

It is fair to say that Calvin did not place the justification of the sinner at the center of his theology. Granted, he states that the matter of justification is "the main hinge on which religion turns. . . ."[16] Yet his general emphasis centers on something different. Both Reformed and Lutheran historians agree that Calvin defined his gospel as the possibility of union with God through Christ.

This emphasis does not contradict Calvin's statements on the meaning or importance of justification. Rather, it takes justification from center stage and places it into the position of being "merely one among several" doctrines of Christianity. In the opening paragraph of his section on justification, Calvin explains this relationship:

> Let us sum these up. Christ was given to us by God's generosity, to be grasped and possessed by us in faith. By partaking of him, we principally receive a double grace: namely, that being reconciled to God through Christ's blamelessness, we

---

[15]See especially Francis Pieper, *Christian Dogmatics,* 4 vols. (Saint Louis: Concordia, 1950). Pieper includes good discussions of Reformed theology in all sections of his book.

[16]Calvin, *Institutes,* p. 726.

> may have in heaven instead of a Judge a gracious Father; and secondly, that sanctified by Christ's spirit we may cultivate blamelessness and purity of life.[17]

Two things stand out in this quotation. First, justification comes as a result of being united with Christ. (Luther would say that we become united with Christ by faith in his justifying us.) Second, the sanctification that comes as a result of being united with Christ is made coordinate with justification instead of dependent on it.

This change in the order of salvation is noted by theologians who affirm that Calvin centers his gospel on union with Christ. Wilhelm Niesel writes:

> Thus for both Calvin and the Heidelberg Catechism, "that joining together of Head and members, that indwelling of Christ in our hearts—in short, that mystical union" is fundamental. "We do not, therefore, contemplate him outside ourselves from afar in order that his righteousness may be imputed to us but because we put on Christ and are engrafted into his body—in short, because he deigns to make us one with him. For this reason, we glory that we have fellowship of righteousness with him." (*Institutes,* III.11.10)[18]

For Luther, Christ's righteous life, his atoning sacrifice, and his resurrection from the dead form the gospel through which God works in us. When we believe that God has justified us, Christ comes to dwell within us. For Calvin, God works faith in his benevolence and love, and through this faith Christ comes to us and gives us

---

[17]Ibid., p. 725.

[18]Wilhelm Niesel, *The Gospel and the Churches* (Philadelphia: Westminster, 1962), p. 182.

his gifts of sanctification and justification. (Note that Luther's order is a logical order rather than a temporal one. Therefore, Luther can also speak about Christ's coming to us with his gifts of salvation. It is this most important logical order that the Reformed churches do not recognize.)

Another Reformed writer, Donald Bloesch, approves of this shift from Luther,

> It remained for Calvin to give due recognition to the pursuit of holiness. Whereas for Luther the dominant motif was the justification of the ungodly, for Calvin the pervading concern was the Christian life. Nonetheless, he too saw the forensic justification as the foundation of the holy life, *but the purpose and goal of justification is perfection in holiness.* (emphasis mine)[19]

In this statement by Bloesch, we begin to see the reason for the difference between Luther and Calvin. Whereas Luther's religion centered on his desire to find a gracious God, Calvin's religion—without denying that forgiveness is important—centered on a desire to become holy. It was this mixture of motives on Calvin's part that led to the shift in emphasis we will continue to develop in the remainder of Part One of our book.

We turn to the observations of an Anglican writer, Alister McGrath, who clearly states the point I am trying to make:

> It will, however, be clear that Calvin is actually concerned not so much with justification, as with incorporation into Christ (which has, as one of its necessary consequences, justification). It is this

---

[19]Donald Bloesch, *Essentials of Evangelical Theology,* vol. 2 (New York: Harper and Row, 1979), p. 36.

45

point which goes some considerable way towards explaining the lack of importance which Calvin appears to attach to justification in the *1559 Institutio.*

It is a well known fact that, in the 1559 edition of this work, Calvin defers his discussion of justification until Book III, and it is then found only after a detailed exposition of sanctification. This has proved a serious embarrassment to those who project Luther's concern with the *articulus iustificationis* on to Calvin, asserting that justification is the "focal centre" of the Institutio. In fact, Calvin's concern is with the manner in which the individual is incorporated into Christ, and the personal and corporate consequences of this *insitio in Christum*—of which justification is but one.[20]

Martin Luther saw that the gospel was the message of forgiveness in Christ. For him, the gospel was an objective fact and as such it was something to be believed. Once a person believed that fact, the door to heaven was opened, the person was a child of God, and *for the first time* he found a desire to serve God.

John Calvin rejoiced in the union with Christ that faith achieved. Such a union enabled him to serve God and to be assured he was justified. We see in him the beginnings of a shift in emphasis that has led churches to consider the gospel as the general means through which God makes us righteous, rather than the more specific message that in Christ God has declared us righteous.

While Calvin had a high regard for God's sovereign grace, his emphasis on grace being an infused quality, in

---

[20]Alister McGrath, *Iustitia Dei,* vol. 2 (Cambridge: Cambridge University Press, 1986), p. 38.

my opinion, was conducive for the future Arminian emphasis. Arminianism asserts that natural man has a certain indwelling desire to become righteous; the decision "to receive Christ into him" brings man the sought after infusion of virtue.

This tendency of John Calvin has gained momentum over the years, producing a Evangelical/Reformed theology that in most denominations has moved far beyond Calvin. Such theology is the seedbed of the Church Growth Movement.

The gospel in contemporary Reformed theology

Much has happened since the Reformation. Yet, basically, the church has not moved beyond the main themes of that most important period. While various theologians have modified and challenged many of the teachings that were accepted at that time, the question of "What is the gospel?" has been asked and answered in various ways. The answers lie somewhere along a continuum that, on the one end, describes Jesus' work as centering in a moral change or, on the other end, in forgiveness.

As we have defined Lutheranism, it views the goal of religion as forgiveness for the sinner. This forgiveness comes to him only when he has come face to face with God's law and despairs of his own righteousness. To what extent is this teaching still taught in the world today? A pat answer cannot be given. Much of Lutheranism today has exchanged the Lutheran understanding of gospel for the Reformed understanding. For them, the gospel has become the tool for the regeneration of humankind either on a personal or societal level.

In the past, many churches of the American Lutheran Church (ALC) still held to the Lutheran understanding. The largest block of churches that held to it were those of the Synodical Conference, composed of the Lutheran Church—Missouri Synod (LCMS), the Wisconsin Synod

(WELS, of which I am a member), and the Evangelical Lutheran Synod (ELS).

With the demise of the Synodical Conference in the early 1960s, one might argue that some in the Missouri Synod have made a shift toward the Reformed emphasis. This is true in spite of the fact that many LCMS churches continue to hold to their traditional stance. The WELS and ELS today are wrestling with these issues and as of this writing remain united around the proclamation of God's general forgiveness of the world, calling people to faith in God's forgiveness and through it to the hope of eternal life. For the most part, though, conservative Lutheranism is a dim light.

Examples from Reformed theology

Through a collage of examples, we will see that Evangelical/Reformed churches today do indeed center their understanding of the gospel on its meeting man's need for moral change.

Henry Hamann, a Missouri Synod pastor and teacher, describes the meaning of justification by faith in modern theology. He concludes that the Reformed (and many Lutherans) make two errors. They either equate justification with regeneration, or they make justification peripheral to regeneration.[21] Hamann cites authors (e.g., C. H. Dodd, Vincent Taylor, James Stewart, Emil Brunner) who are quoted more by mainline liberal teachers and perhaps neo-evangelicals than by conser-

---

[21]Henry Hamann, "Justification by Faith in Modern Theology" (Th.D. dissertation, Concordia Theological Seminary, 1956), pp. v,vi. The use of the term "regeneration" here might tend to confuse the issue, although I see no way of getting around it. The gospel does indeed lead to regeneration, the "new birth." However, when used as a contrast to justification in discussions about Lutheran vs. Reformed theology, the term is often used to denote the emphasis toward renewal of life, or increased morality apart from a gospel motivation. That is how it is used here, following the way Henry Hamann has used it in his book.

vative Evangelicals, but he includes a quotation by the popular and more conservative C. S. Lewis to support his thesis.

In the following quotation, notice how C. S. Lewis equates regeneration with justification. He describes the natural human life as a life of self-centeredness and autonomous pride, and then describes the kind of life that Jesus led—the complete opposite. He "killed his human desires at every turn," and the result was that now "we see a *real* man."[22] Lewis continues:

> Now what *is* the difference which he has made to the whole human mass? It is just this: that the business of becoming a son of God, of being turned from a created into a begotten thing, of passing over from the temporary biological life into the timeless "spiritual" life, has been done for us. Humanity is already "saved" in principle. . . . We haven't got to try to climb up into spiritual life by our own efforts: it has already come down into the human race. If we will only lay ourselves open to the one Man in whom it was fully present, . . . He will do it in us and for us.

> Of course, you can express this in all sorts of different ways. You can say that Christ died for your sins. You may say that the Father has forgiven us because Christ has done for us what we ought to have done. You may say that you are washed in the blood of the Lamb. . . . They're all true. If any of them don't appeal to you, leave it alone and get on with the formula that does."[23]

---

[22]C. S. Lewis, *Beyond Personality* (New York: The MacMillan Company, 1945), pp. 28-31, quoted in Henry Hamann, op. cit., p. 46.

[23]Ibid.

This is only one quotation from a man who wrote much. But it is a good example of equating forgiveness (justification) with the new creation (regeneration). Lewis cites as the condition, "If we will only lay ourselves open." The result will follow, "He will do it." Becoming another type of man is the goal. Christ's becoming that man through his life is the tool. Opening ourselves to an infusion of his power to make us like him is the goal achieved.

Hamann quotes other authors to the same effect. One of them is James S. Stewart:

> The sinful soul, confronted with God's wonderful self-disclosure in Christ, and with the tremendous and subduing fact of the cross where the whole world's sins were borne, responds to that divine appeal and abandons itself to the love that stands revealed: and that response, that abandonment, Paul calls faith. This is what God sees when He justifies the ungodly.[24]

This quotation demonstrates a characteristic of conversion in the context of the "infused grace" model. The love of God is the drawing force. But instead of the love of God in Christ that centers on Christ's work of atonement and that draws men through the knowledge of forgiveness, this love is a general love that draws a response of love, much the same as human love does.

This is important, for it is on this somewhat general love of God that many evangelism methods are based.[25]

---

[24]James S. Stewart, *A Man in Christ* (New York: Harper and Brothers, n.d.) p. 256, quoted in Henry Hamann, op. cit., p. 47.

[25]For example, see the widely used "Four Spiritual Laws" approach of Campus Crusade. The point of contact is that God has a plan for your life. Through repentance and faith a person can get on God's track and experience the outworking of this plan. In this scheme, the love of God is altered from a

Hamann quotes other authors to prove his point. He cites Paul Holmer, "To justify your ideas you must think and know; to justify your life you must transform it,"[26] and Jacques Maritain, "The justice received through faith . . . is a justice bestowed, continually bestowed, a flowering within us of the life of Christ, a vitalizing by his blood."[27]

Hamann's second point is that justification is often made a peripheral matter. This more accurately describes the modern Evangelicals. David Hesselgrave, a missiologist teaching at Trinity Seminary, Deerfield, Illinois, discusses the importance of forgiveness in his book on cross-cultural church planting:

> Conversion is an act of the believer which follows repentance in which he turns to God in such a fashion that the beliefs and practices of the old religion are completely forsaken and the grace of God becomes observable in his life. . . . First, conversion is important because it is a prerequisite to blessing (Acts 3:19). Second, conversion is important because it naturally precedes service to God (1 Thess. 1:9,10). Third, in that conversion is outward and observable, it is important to the Christian witness. *Fourth, conversion is important because it is related to forgiveness of sins* (Acts 3:19; 26:18). . . . Fifth, conversion is impor-

---

love that is centered in Christ's forgiveness (which only a knowledge of the law and sin can lead a person to appreciate) to a general love that is aimed at helping a person in his life. In the first view, God's love is acquired by contrition and faith, while in the latter view it is acquired by turning from sin. We will speak more of this in chapter 8.

[26]Paul L. Holmer, "Law and Gospel Reexamined," *Theology Today* (January 1954), pp. 447ff., quoted in Henry Hamann, op. cit., p. 49.

[27]Jacques Maritain, *The Living Thoughts of Saint Paul,* trans. Henry Binsse (London: Cassell and Company, Ltd., 1942), pp. 52ff., quoted in Henry Hamann, op. cit., p. 49.

tant because it is related to the law. (emphasis mine)[28]

Note in the above quotation how forgiveness is not central in conversion. Conversion has more to do with a general sort of regeneration than with forgiveness, although forgiveness is certainly listed as one of the outcomes.

One of the things I watched for during the class sessions at Fuller Seminary, and in the reading assignments, was the relative importance given to the forgiveness of sins. Although it is hard to document a lack of something in a large body of writing and lectures, it's my conclusion that the emphasis on God's judgment over man's sins, and the hope of God's glory that Christ won for us through his atonement, is indeed a peripheral issue in neo-evangelical writing and in Church Growth literature in particular. Occasionally the gospel is defined; more often it is only assumed.

A few examples will help us see that when the gospel is discussed, it relates more to regeneration than to justification. Donald McGavran describes evangelism: "Church-growth principles say, 'Engage in evangelism, confronting people with the commands of Christ.'"[29] In a more extended discussion of evangelism and conversion, Donald McGavran and Win Arn write:

> The Church Growth Movement is based on solid conviction. Christ has spoken the definitive and final work: "I am the way, I am the truth, I am the life. No man comes to the Father but by me."

---

[28]David J. Hesselgrave, *Planting Churches Cross-Culturally: A Guide for Home and Foreign Missions* (Grand Rapids: Baker Book House, 1980), pp. 235,236.

[29]Donald A. McGavran and Win Arn, *How to Grow a Church* (Ventura, Calif.: Regal Books, 1973), p. 162.

... What does it mean to believe in the Name of Jesus Christ?

To believe in the Name of Jesus Christ means at least three acts. First, intellectual acceptance. We move from ignorance or doubt to an acceptance of truth: that "Jesus" is the mighty Name—the only Name. That God has willed to reveal himself through Jesus Christ, his Word made flesh, Jesus who upholds "the universe by his Word of power."

Second, since Jesus is Lord, and I accept this intellectually, I submit my entire life to him. I obey him in every command he gives me. He is *my* Lord. I subject all my actions, thoughts, attitudes and values, expenditure of time and money to Jesus Christ. I treat my fellow men as Christ commands. I try to create a family, community, business, and state which would please him. I accept what the Bible so clearly says, again and again, that the whole life of the Christian has been transformed. He is therefore a new creation . . . .

A third meaning of belief is that I must share the good news with others.[30]

What McGavran and Arn say is true, but it's also clear from this passage that they do not see forgiveness as a very important part of faith. Nowhere is it mentioned—and the section I quoted is the only place in the book where there is anything resembling a definition of faith! Faith is a moral commitment to God. Moral regeneration takes precedence over justification.

We won't carry the discussion of the gospel in the Church Growth Movement any further right now. In Part Two, where we will examine the methods of the

---

[30]Donald McGavran and Win Arn, *Back to Basics in Church Growth* (Wheaton, Ill.: Tyndale, 1981), p. 52.

Church Growth Movement, we will have occasion again to touch base with their understanding of the gospel. From this discussion, however, and from what follows in the next few paragraphs, we can begin to see that the Church Growth movement clearly falls into the Reformed theological camp, both on the nature of the gospel and the nature of the kingdom.

I might add that a Lutheran emphasis on the gospel can be found in some Reformed churches. My wife, who came to faith in the Evangelical Free Church and whose youth pastor was a student at Trinity Seminary, Deerfield, noted a strong emphasis on grace and forgiveness in his teaching. Later, when she considered Lutheranism, she simply saw that what we taught in the Lutheran church was what she had been told by her youth pastor, but it was presented in a more consistent way.

In the Theology of Church Growth class, I asked Eddie Gibbs for his definition of the gospel. He surprised me with a fine confession in which he centered his understanding of the gospel squarely on the forgiveness of sins that God gives to undeserving sinners. I say I was surprised, because the message of forgiveness played a rather minimal role in the discussions of that class, as well as in the other sessions I attended at Fuller Seminary.

We could cite other examples of Reformed authors describing the gospel as objective justification.[31] But the shift in emphasis is clear, and it continues to play a dominant role in the tension between conservative Lutheranism and the Reformed churches.

---

[31]An interesting example of this is in Carl Henry, ed., *Christian Faith and Modern Theology* (New York: Channel Press, 1964), pp. 348ff. In this book that deals with various doctrines of Christianity written primarily by Reformed authors, a professor at Concordia Seminary, Springfield (LCMS) was chosen to write the article on justification. It is a fine article pointing out the nature of objective justification, and centering justification on the forgiveness of sins. But I wonder how many Evangelicals who read the article fully agreed with it.

5.

THE KINGDOM OF GOD—
LUTHERAN AND REFORMED

The point we made about the shift in theology from Martin Luther to John Calvin finds expression also in their understanding of the kingdom of God. In the Bible, the "kingdom of God" is synonymous with the gospel of God's forgiveness working in the hearts of its hearers.[1] The value of studying the meaning of the gospel under the heading of the kingdom of God is that this term denotes something that God is doing among us.

Just what is God doing among us? In seeking to answer this question, we find the same shift in emphasis as we discussed in chapter 4.

---

[1] Cf. Matthew 4:23 and Luke 8:1, "good news of the kingdom" (NIV).

Martin Luther's understanding of the kingdom of God

Luther's understanding of the kingdom of God parallels his understanding of justification. As we look at several statements by Luther on the kingdom of God, we will note God's activity of forgiving the sins of the world and of working faith in the hearts of people to believe in that forgiveness. This work is the central activity God carries out as King.

Luther's Genesis commentaries furnish some good examples of this. In a discussion of Abraham's home life, he wrote:

> Consequently the Word of God is continually heard there, and Abraham's home is nothing else than a kingdom of forgiveness of sins and of grace, yes, a very heaven in which dwell the angels of God, whom he receives reverently. In short, in Abraham's home there is nothing but grace and life.[2]

In another section, we note this same emphasis on the forgiveness of sins:

> Then the Lord says, "I pardon you freely, without any merits on your part. I shall do this when I forgive you your sins: I shall make you an heir and child of the kingdom of God, that I may declare My love toward you in such a way that I first wash away your filth. First I must wipe and wash you." Thus a mother does not put her baby into a cradle without first washing and cleansing it. Nor does the baby's wailing and weeping pre-

---

[2]Martin Luther, *Luther's Works,* ed. Jaroslav Pelikan, vol. 5 (Saint Louis: Concordia, 1968), p. 228.

vent her from washing it. Thus we have been called to the kingdom of God. We have the remission of sin. We are children and heirs of God.[3]

The link between the Word of God and the kingdom of God is clear. Commenting on Genesis 49:10, Luther wrote:

In the Word, therefore, is a most powerful kingdom against death, sin and the devil, and all their tyranny, with power to save, to set free, and to defend for eternal salvation. . . . Thus Christ says: "Go into all the world and preach the gospel to the whole creation." (Mark 16:15) To this king the nations shall listen; that is, they will be ruled by the Word. The work will be done through preachings. . . . I absolve you; I baptize you; I declare you to be a child of the kingdom; I announce to you the remission of sins; I promise and offer you victory over the devil. Believe and you will be saved.[4]

By the Word, Luther obviously means the gospel. God's Word contains the law also, and the law has no place in our receiving God's kingdom other than to prepare us for it. Hence, the proper use of law and gospel is vital in bringing the kingdom of God to people through the preaching of the Word. In a sermon on a text from John's Gospel, Luther states:

This story [the woman caught in adultery] is related to show the clear distinction between the law and the gospel, or between the kingdom of Christ and that of the world. The Pharisees had

---

[3]Luther, *Luther's Works*, vol. 7, p. 234.
[4]Luther, *Luther's Works*, vol. 8, p. 244.

heard that Christ had preached much about the kingdom of God in his sermons, stating that it was a kingdom of grace in which forgiveness of sin held sway. In Christ's realm no punishment is to be found, but only mercy and forgiveness of sins, whereas in the realm of Moses and the world there is no forgiveness of sins, but only wrath and punishment.[5]

In an important statement, Luther states that a person must realize his need for forgiveness in order to enter the kingdom. Luther wrote:

Thus the kingdom of Christ concerns itself with sinners who feel their sins and are tortured, tormented, and frightened by them, with those whose heart feels death.[6]

Thus only sinners belong in the kingdom of Christ who recognize their sin, feel it, and then catch hold of the word spoken here: "I do not condemn you." These people constitute the membership of Christ's kingdom.[7]

To relate this to the discussion in the previous two chapters, it is not the desire to become righteous, but the terror of standing before God in our own unrighteousness, that is the spiritual posture necessary before one can believe the Word and through the gospel enter the kingdom. Luther is clear that the fruits of the kingdom are not the kingdom itself:

This too is a new distinction by which Christ's kingdom is distinguished from the kingdoms of

---

[5]Luther, *Luther's Works,* vol. 23, p. 310.

[6]Ibid., p. 317.

[7]Ibid., p. 318.

the world, where there is hatred or unrighteousness even when everything prospers well. In Christ's kingdom there is true love of righteousness because the Word is pure; it permits no jesting but teaches the purest faith and warns us to flee vices.[8]

Note the distinction. The kingdom of God produces sanctification, but is not the sanctification itself. This is crucial to our understanding of the nature of the gospel and to our discussion of the difference between Luther and Calvin. We will return to this point when we consider Calvin's understanding of the kingdom.

We offer one final quotation from Luther. It is in his *Large Catechism,* where he explains the meaning of the Second Petition of the Lord's Prayer. This quotation will enable us to draw a contrast with Calvin as we examine his explanation of this same petition. Luther wrote:

But what is the kingdom of God? Answer: Nothing else than what we learned in the Creed, that God sent His Son Jesus Christ, our Lord, into the world to redeem and deliver us from the power of the devil, and to bring us to Himself, and to govern us as a King of righteousness, life, and salvation against sin, death, and an evil conscience, for which end He has also bestowed His Holy Ghost, who is to bring these things home to us by His holy Word, and to illumine and strengthen us in the faith by his power.[9]

---

[8]Luther, *Luther's Works,* vol. 12, p. 245.

[9]Martin Luther, *The Concordia Triglotta* (Saint Louis: Concordia, 1921), p. 711.

John Calvin's understanding of the kingdom of God

For the most part, Calvin, like Luther, talks about the kingdom of God in an incidental way as he discusses other subjects. Two subject headings, however, give us a good opportunity to discover how Calvin defines the kingdom of God: the Second Petition of the Lord's Prayer, and the three offices of Christ. A reading of these sections in his Institutes will show similarities between Luther and Calvin, but they will also show a distinct and significant difference.

While the statements of Luther on the Second Petition and the kingdom of God are fresh in our minds, it would be well to read what Calvin has to say about the same subject. In a section where we would expect to find his clearest definition of the kingdom of God, we find only a statement to the effect that in God's kingdom he shapes our wills to parallel his:

> But even though the definition of this kingdom was put before us previously, I now briefly repeat it: God reigns where men, both by denial of themselves and by contempt of the world and of earthly life, pledge themselves to his righteousness in order to aspire to a heavenly life. Thus there are two parts to this kingdom: first that God by the power of his Spirit corrects all the desires of the flesh which by squadrons war against him; second, that he shapes all our thoughts in obedience to his rule.[10]

Calvin refers to another place where he had "previously" spoken about the kingdom of God. In this other

---

[10]John Calvin, *Institutes of the Christian Religion*, The Library of Christian Classics, vol. 20 (Philadelphia: Westminster, 1960), pp. 498,499.

passage, he is much closer to Luther and does not separate the sacrifice of Christ from the kingdom:

> John, a messenger sent before the face of Christ to prepare his ways proclaimed, "Repent for the kingdom of Heaven has come near." *By inviting them to repentance, he admonished them to recognize that they were sinners, and their all was condemned before the Lord, that they might with all their hearts desire the mortification of the flesh, and a new rebirth in the Spirit. By proclaiming the kingdom of God, he was calling them to faith, for by the kingdom of God, which he taught was at hand, he meant the forgiveness of sins, salvation, life, and utterly everything that we obtain in Christ* . . . . What else is this than that they, weighed down and wearied by the burden of sins, should turn to the Lord and conceive a hope of forgiveness and salvation. (emphasis mine)[11]

At best, then, Calvin presents us with a mixed understanding of the kingdom. In the second italicized sentence in the quotation above, he speaks almost like Luther speaks. But in the first italicized sentence he presents the teaching of John the Baptist as a call to "desire the mortification of the flesh" and "desire a new rebirth." In the second statement he conceives of the gospel as God's declaration of forgiveness, but in the first, as an infusion of power leading to holiness of life.

The other section of Calvin's writings that sheds light on his understanding of the kingdom is his discussion of the three offices of Christ.[12] When Calvin discusses the three offices of Christ, he lists the offices as prophet, king, and priest. This probably would not strike a non-

[11]Ibid., p. 613.
[12]Ibid., pp. 498ff.

Lutheran as unusual, but a Lutheran notices a difference in the order in which Calvin lists these offices. Luther spoke about Christ's three offices as prophet, priest, and king. I believe that here we have another indication of the basic difference between the two reformers.

As we've seen, Luther based his understanding of the kingdom of God on the fact that its King was the Lamb of God, who as a Priest had sacrificed himself for the sins of the world and who built his kingdom on that message. Calvin, on the other hand, viewed Christ as a Priest because he is first the King who had all things under his control, and as King accomplished the sacrifice necessary to save mankind.

Luther would agree that only the supreme God could provide the necessary sacrifice for mankind. But the effect of Calvin's change of order is to place the sovereign God at the center and shift the cross to the side. Why does Calvin do this? I will venture an opinion on which I will continue to expand: A person who is concerned with becoming holy in this life will automatically place a greater importance on submitting to the will of a Sovereign God than he will place on Jesus' sacrifice for him. Christ's office of King becomes more important for him than his office of Priest. And Christ's priestly office becomes merely the way in which God provided the means for man to come under his moral influence.

Simply put, to Calvin, Christ's work as Priest is done because he is a King. To Luther, Christ becomes our King because he first has been our Priest. (Luther would acknowledge the fact that God exercises a general kingship over all things, but emphatically states that this aspect of his kingdom is a hidden kingdom. In his Word, though, God's kingdom is revealed to us—not based on his sovereignty but on his atonement for our sins. He has become our King only after his sacrifice has made it possible that as the powerful King of all he can shower his blessings on us and be our King even though we are sinners.)

It is only natural that in Calvin's discussion of Christ's work as King, he speaks in more general terms than Luther about the aid and help our King gives us in our fight of faith. The forgiveness of sins plays an important part, but not the central role as in Luther.

Calvin recognizes that Christ's kingdom is not a matter of outward appearances. (And Calvin was as insistent as Luther that being a Christian brings trouble and hardship.) He says:

> In like manner Christ enriches his people with all things necessary for the eternal salvation of souls and fortifies them with courage to stand unconquerable against all the assaults of the spiritual enemies. Hence we are furnished, as far as God knows to be expedient for us, with the gifts of the Spirit which we lack by nature. By these first fruits we may perceive that we are truly joined to God in perfect blessedness. Then relying upon the power of the same Spirit, let us not doubt that we shall always be victorious over the devil, the world, and every kind of harmful thing.

> Thus it is that we patiently pass through this life with its misery, hunger, cold, contempt, reproaches, and other troubles—content with this one thing: that our King will never leave us destitute, but will provide for our needs until, our warfare ended, we are called to triumph. *Such is the nature of his rule,* that he shares with us all that he has received from the Father. Now he arms and equips us with his power, adorns us with his beauty and magnificence, enriches us with his wealth. These benefits, then, give us the most

> fruitful occasion to glory, and also provide us
> with confidence to struggle fearlessly against the
> devil, sin, and death. (emphasis mine)[13]

These words are good words. They could have been spoken by Luther. But the fact is that Calvin bases his hope in Christ as a "bare" King—that is, as a King who is not wrapped up in his atoning work for us. Not until the last sentence of this section does Calvin state, "Finally, clothed with his righteousness, we can valiantly rise above all the world's reproaches; and just as he himself freely lavishes his gifts upon us, so may we, in return, bring forth fruit to his glory."[14]

Here we finally have mention of Christ's righteousness as his gift to us. Again, we see that Calvin presents us with a mixed understanding of the kingdom. On the one hand, he presents us with a kingdom based on Christ's humiliation. On the other hand, he presents us with a more diffused sort of kingdom in which God is interested primarily in preserving and increasing the morality of his church through his grace. What increases the confusion is that in the two sections of his work where we would expect the more focused definition of the kingdom, we find a very general one.

As we look ahead to our discussion of the ministry of outreach and the ministry of the church in general, we note that Calvin's diffused definition of the kingdom— and, as we have seen, of the gospel—will have practical consequences. Luther's understanding of the kingdom of God as based on the priestly work of Christ leads to a more focused ministry and outreach. Calvin's more diffused understanding of the kingdom leads to a more general type of ministry, in which God's love and power

---

[13]Ibid., pp. 498,499.

[14]Ibid., p. 499.

are stressed with a diminished emphasis on the guilt of sin and Christ's sacrifice for it.

The kingdom of God
in contemporary Reformed theology

The meaning of the Kingdom of God in current Reformed theology is an extension of the pattern begun by Calvin. C. H. Dodd has had considerable influence on mainline Protestantism, and he was quoted favorably at the Fuller Seminary Church Growth II lectures. His understanding of the kingdom is consistent with the "infused grace" model. For Dodd, the presence of the kingdom in the world means that God is calling people to decide for him and follow his ways. In the closing paragraphs of his well known book *The Parables of the Kingdom,* Dodd writes,

> We have, it appears, no warrant in the teaching of Jesus for affirming that the long cycles of history will lead inevitably to a millennial "Kingdom Come" on earth. But we have warrant for affirming that God comes to meet us in history and sets before us the open but narrow door into his Kingdom. To accept His Kingdom and to enter in brings blessedness, because the best conceivable thing is that we should be in obedience to the will of God. Such blessedness may be enjoyed here and now, but it is never exhausted in any experience that falls within the bounds of time and space. Our destiny lies in the eternal order.[15]

For Dodd, the "eternal order" does not refer to an eternal life in heaven. Rather, it refers to the grace of

---

[15]C. H. Dodd, *The Parables of the Kingdom* (London: Nisbet, 1936), p. 169.

God which has made this world "alive with divine energies."[16]

The Evangelical/Reformed world is not quite as centered on the here and now as Dodd is, but its understanding of the kingdom of God tends to place a premium on the empirical results of God's activity here and now. In other words, if the cumulative results of God's regenerating activity in the Christian can be seen in society, then the kingdom has come.

Dispensationalist writers claim that the kingdom should have come during Christ's lifetime, but because most of the people rejected him, he postponed the kingdom until a later time. William Hoyt, a dispensational writer, begins his discussion of the kingdom with God's command to man to rule over the earth. He sees this as the theme that recurs in the Bible until "at last the throne of God is established on earth."[17] While Christ made a bid to bring this to pass, he was rejected.

According to Hoyt, the purpose of the present church age is to "form an aristocracy for the kingdom."[18] This aristocracy is composed of Christians and will rule with Christ in the final coming of the kingdom. For now, though, "In a limited sense, members of the church experience participation in this kingdom today."[19] Hoyt writes, "We have failed because we turned our faces from God. But we succeed by the power of God in the conquering of disease, the prevention of some wars, the adding of years to the span of life, the elimination of some social and political ills."[20]

---

[16]Ibid., p. 158.

[17]Herman Hoyt, "Dispensational Premillennialism," *The Meaning of the Millennium,* ed. Robert Clouse (Downer's Grove: IVP, 1977), p. 64.

[18]Ibid., p. 90.

[19]Ibid.

[20]Ibid., p. 68.

Hoyt rightly claims that Christians are members of Christ's kingdom before its final consummation in glory. But his understanding of the nature of the kingdom tends to make the status of Christians in relation to the kingdom ambiguous. Like the more liberal C. H. Dodd, Hoyt views Christ's kingdom as one of morals and the fruits of morality. Hence this kingdom is in doubt unless there is empirical evidence to support its existence.

Another group concerned about the empirical data is that of the Pentecostal/Charismatics. Concerning the kingdom of God, John Wimber states:

> In order to fully understand the validity of a Signs and Wonders ministry, we need to study the concept of the Kingdom of God. The Kingdom of God is the Rule of God (the age to come) which has invaded the kingdom (rule) of Satan (this present evil Age), and is the arena in which Signs and Wonders occur. They are the "marks" (Signs) of the Kingdom. Understanding about the Kingdom of God is fundamental to understanding the ministry of Jesus; the kingdom of Satan was his real enemy. There was a war going on! Jesus was sent by God to shatter the strongholds of Satan. His one purpose was Satan's defeat. Jesus accomplished this through his death, resurrection, and ascension. This demonstrated who was the victor, but Satan is not yet cast out and will not be until Christ returns to establish his Kingdom forever. The Church is God's army in the continual fight which goes on with Satan as she lives "between the times."[21]

---

[21]John Wimber, "Signs and Wonder," Class Notes for Church Growth II, Fuller Theological Seminary (1987), p. 7.

Wimber's understanding of the kingdom revolves around the evidence for it. It is a kingdom that he holds to be in existence by faith, but since he equates the kingdom with evidence, the incomplete evidence of modern signs and miracles demonstrates to him that the kingdom is only partially operative right now.

Peter Wagner has the same emphasis, "The kingdom of Satan has been definitively invaded by the kingdom of God."[22] And Eddie Gibbs writes, "In the subsequent experience of the Church in exercising this ministry there have been many instances of failure, partial, delayed and temporary healing, reminding us that we live with the tension of the 'now' and the 'not yet' of the kingdom."[23]

Even more conservative Evangelical authors, although they leave room for "spiritualization" of the kingdom, cannot shake completely the desire to focus on the evidence. George Peters of Trinity Seminary, Deerfield, Illinois, discusses the kingdom of God in his book, *A Theology of Church Growth*. While he speaks about the kingdom of God in spiritual terms, he equates entry into it not with justification but with regeneration. He writes, "It is the sphere that can be entered by sinful man only by means of personal regeneration by the Spirit through a faith relationship with Jesus Christ."[24]

George Ladd holds the same view. He successfully argues with the liberals and equates the kingdom of God with God's "redemptive rule, now present in the person, deeds, and words of Jesus."[25] But Ladd also views the

---

[22]C. Peter Wagner, *Spiritual Power and Church Growth* (Altamonte Springs, Fla.: Strang Communications, 1986), p. 38.

[23]Eddie Gibbs, *I Believe in Church Growth* (Grand Rapids: Eerdmans, 1981), p. 68.

[24]George Peters, *A Theology of Church Growth* (Grand Rapids: Zondervan, 1981), p. 40.

[25]George Ladd, *Jesus and the Kingdom* (Waco: Word Books, 1964), p. 165.

kingdom as the moral effects of God's rule. When he views the world within that context, he must conclude, "We need not think of this victory of the kingdom as a complete defeat of Satan. Indeed this idea can hardly be entertained, for Satan continues to be active in the subsequent ministry of Jesus."[26]

George Peters likewise concludes, "Thus while the church is realized eschatology and realized kingdom of God, it is so in part only and its limitations must be recognized and appreciated."[27]

Luther understood the kingdom to be God's working with his grace by winning salvation, bestowing salvation on his people, and judging the guilty. The above theologies see it more as the effects of God's overcoming the results of sin according to his power as King. Interpreting the *results* of the kingdom as if they were the kingdom itself lies at the bottom of what we see happening in twentieth century interpretation.

Conclusion

The shift that began in Calvin's writings has continued and gained momentum over the centuries. The emphasis on union with Christ, the idea that the center of Christianity lies in the empirical results of God's making a person righteous, and the understanding of the kingdom of God as a rule in which he changes the individual or society, has gained momentum.

This emphasis finds expression in Church Growth methods, as we will see in Part Two.

---

[26]Ladd, op. cit., p. 148. Note that in the same paragraph Ladd says, "The figures of the binding and disarming of Satan are metaphors describing a spiritual reality. The powers of God's Kingdom have invaded human history. The power of evil has been defeated." This results in a rather confusing picture of Satan's status. Is he defeated or is he only partially defeated?

[27]Peters, *A Theology of Church Growth,* p. 43.

6.

THE GOSPEL AND CONVERSION

No matter how great a theologian might be, on a certain level he is the same as everyone else. For all the complexities of theology, the theologian still lives and breathes as the layman does. His mind may be filled with subtle distinctions, but his spirit lives on the very simple level of the relative place he gives to forgiveness and moral improvement in his conception of Christianity. The way he adjusts his priorities is influenced largely through his conversion experience. As he grows, he either affirms or denies elements of his conversion experience and shapes his theology and methodology accordingly.

The distinction we have made between Luther and Calvin becomes quite vivid when we look at the types of conversion experiences that spring from their theologies and that, in turn, foster methods of ministry that perpetuate both the experience and the theology.

The nature of conversion

The nature of the Christian conversion experience is largely hidden from our view. Jesus compares the work of the Holy Spirit to the wind that "blows wherever it pleases. You hear its sound, but you cannot tell where it comes from or where it is going. So it is with everyone born of the Spirit" (John 3:7,8). Trying to analyze individual conversion experiences may be presumptuous; it could lead one into the dangerous area of judging hearts.

Nonetheless, if we look at conversion throughout the religious world, we soon realize that there are all sorts of conversion experiences. Non-Christians experience religious conversions in which their perception of the world and their object of worship is changed. Members of cults and pseudo-religious groups also have conversion experiences in which they experience something they interpret as God leading them to espouse a new faith. Whether we like it or not, we are forced to make decisions about the validity of a person's conversion experience, just as we are forced to make judgments about the validity of the body of teaching that he or she believes.

As we think about evangelism work, and about the growth of the church in general, we must ask ourselves this question: "If there are conversion experiences linked with all types of religion, then how can I be sure that I lead my hearer in a direction where his conversion to God will be genuine and based on the truth?" The answer to that question, of course, is to speak the truth and let the truth do its work. Specifically, it means presenting the law and the gospel in such a way that people are led to know the guilt of their sin, and believe that their hope of God's forgiveness lies in Christ.

Sadly, the difference between the Lutheran understanding of the gospel and the kingdom of God, and that of the Evangelical/Reformed, is also evident in their respective conversions. (The chart in Appendix B

71

illustrates this difference.) Of course, we should never imagine that all is black and white. Both a false conversion and a true conversion can take place at the same time, as long as the message of God's forgiveness is present.

In this chapter we will look at several conversion experiences. They serve to illustrate the nature of conversion in the church at large and help us come to grips with the difference between Lutheran and Reformed theology.

I beg the reader's indulgence as I include long quotations in the text. I see no other way of enabling the reader to get a feel for these experiences unless I let the subject speak for himself.

Saint Augustine's conversion

Admittedly, the first man we examine is outside the scope of the two churches we are trying to compare. Including him may be helpful, however, since his conversion forms a striking contrast to Luther's and helps us understand one of the characteristics of a more Reformed type of conversion—namely, that one type of conversion is triggered by reading a command of God rather than a promise of God.

Including Augustine will also enable us to see that the phenomenon I am describing is one that has been felt in the church from its beginning. It is not just associated with Lutherans and Evangelical/Reformed people. We can appreciate Augustine's greatness. Yet, his conversion has more in common with a Reformed conversion than with Luther's.

Augustine was an adult convert. He records his conversion experience in his *Confessions,* a remarkable book that allows us to look into the heart of this great church leader. He explains his conversion:

I hesitated to die to death and live to life; inveterate evil had more power over me than the novelty of good, and as that very moment of time in which I was to become something else drew nearer and nearer, it struck me with more and more horror. Toys and trifles, utter vanities had been my mistresses, and now they were holding me back, pulling me by the garment of my flesh and softly murmuring in my ear: "Are you getting rid of us?" and "From this moment shall we never be with you again for all eternity?" My God, what was it, what was it that they suggested in those words "this" or "that" which I have just written? I pray you in your mercy to keep such things from the soul of your servant. How filthy, how shameful were these things they were suggesting! And I was blushing for shame, because I could still hear the dim voices of those vanities, and still I hung back in hesitation. And again she seemed to be speaking: "Stop your ears against those unclean members of yours, so that they may be mortified. They tell you of delights, but not of such delights as the law of the Lord your God tells." So went the controversy in my heart—about self, and self against self.

And now from my hidden depths my searching thought had dragged up and set before the sight of my heart the whole mass of my misery. Then a huge storm rose up within me bringing with it a huge downpour of tears. I flung myself down on the ground somehow under a fig tree and gave free rein to my tears; they streamed and flooded from my eyes, an acceptable sacrifice to Thee. And I kept saying to you, not perhaps in these words, but with this sense: "And Thou, O Lord, how long? How long, Lord: Wilt Thou be angry forever? Remember not our former iniquities." For I felt that it was these which were holding me fast. And in my misery I would exclaim: "How long, how long this 'tomorrow and tomorrow'? Why not now? Why not finish this very hour with my uncleanness?"

[Augustine hears the voice of a girl that tells him to pick up the book (the Bible) and read.] I checked the force of my tears and rose to my feet, Being quite certain that I must interpret this as a divine command to me to open the book and read the first passage which I should come upon. For I had heard this about Antony: he had happened to come in when the gospel was being read, and as though the words read were spoken directly to himself, had received the admonition: Go, sell all that thou hast, and give to the poor, and thou shalt have treasure in heaven, and come and follow me. And by such an oracle he had been immediately converted to you. I snatched up the book, opened it, and read in silence the passage upon which my eyes first fell: Not in rioting and drunkenness, not in chambering and wantonness, not in strife and envying: but put ye on the Lord Jesus Christ, and make not provision for the flesh in concupiscence. I had no wish to read further; there was no need to. For immediately I had reached the end of this sentence it was as though my heart was filled with a light of confidence and all the shadows of my doubt were swept away. For you converted me to you in such a way that I no longer sought a wife nor any other worldly hope. I was now standing on that rule of faith, just as you had shown me to her in a vision so many years before. (Confessions VIII,11,12)[1]

---

[1]Saint Augustine, *The Confessions of Saint Augustine,* trans. Rex Warner (New York: New American Library, 1963), pp. 179-183.

As we read Augustine's conversion we note several points. First, it was a desire for holiness that led to his conversion. He wanted to put off the sins in which he was trapped. He knew there would come a time when he would have to give them up, but they struggled to remain in his heart. Second, he already believed in God. He desired to dedicate himself more fully to him. Third, the passage that caught his eye and that led to his conversion was an instruction of the Lord to put off sin. Within that passage, at least the section quoted by Augustine in his *Confessions,* there was no mention of forgiveness, or the work of Christ for mankind. Fourth, his conversion was followed by a sweet feeling of euphoria which supplanted the desires of his flesh.

What is noteworthy is that in this entire section there is no mention of forgiveness. And yet this experience is what Augustine considered the time of his conversion.

Augustine could have been discussing the conversion experience of any modern day Evangelical and, for that matter, of many Lutherans. Whatever we might think of his conversion, the results of his conversion experience are clear. His faith became a more general sort of faith, a faith that had as much to do with obedience (by God's grace, of course) as it did with God's declaring him guiltless.

In his recent history of the doctrine of justification, Alister McGrath points out that Augustine's teaching on justification did not parallel Luther's. He writes, "Augustine understands the verb *iustificare* to mean 'to make righteous', an understanding of the term which he appears to have held throughout his working life."[2] McGrath also writes, "For Augustine, it is love, rather than faith, which is the power which brings about the conversion of man."[3]

---

[2] Alister McGrath, *Iustitia Dei,* vol. 2 (Cambridge: Cambridge University Press, 1986), p. 17.

[3] Ibid., p. 30.

Alister McGrath credits Augustine with an important idea that was to form the "fountainhead" of later discussions of the nature of justification.[4] He explains, "Man's righteousness, effected in justification, is regarded by Augustine as *inherent* rather than *imputed,* to use the vocabulary of the sixteenth century."[5] He continues, "For Augustine, justification includes both the beginnings of man's righteousness before God and its subsequent perfection, . . . Augustine's fundamental concept of *iustitia* is that of the submission of the individual's whole being to God."[6]

On this score, Calvin would be closer to Augustine than Luther would be. Both Augustine and Calvin were more concerned about the moral effects of Christianity than about treasuring God's forgiveness and keeping it at center stage.

August Franke's conversion

August Franke was at the center of a movement in the Lutheran and Reformed churches that began in a time of ecclesiastical deadness. Men like Franke yearned for the church to be holy, and he was willing to begin with himself. His intense desire to practice what he would preach was at the center of his conversion experience. Note the similarity of his experience to that of Augustine's.

> I have no cause to complain to God because of this situation, for God did not cease often very strongly to stir up my conscience and to call me to repentance through his Word. I was truly convinced that I was not in the proper state. I often cast myself down upon my knees and asked God

---

[4]Ibid., p. 17.
[5]Ibid., p. 31.
[6]Ibid., pp. 32,35.

for improvement. I can say only that for twenty-four years I was nothing better than an unfruitful tree which bears much foliage but for the most part evil fruit.

But in the twenty-fourth year of my life I began to take up this serious question in myself, to acknowledge more deeply my wretched state and to look upon myself with greater earnestness, desiring that my soul might be freed from this state. But completely unnoticed, my heart was stirred by the highest God to humble myself before him, to pray to him for grace, and often to weep upon my knees, asking him to place me in a different life situation and to make me a justified child of God. I had to make a beginning anew to become a Christian.

There was yet a base in my heart that I very much loved godliness and spoke about it earnestly without falsity as well as convincing good friends of my intentions hereafter to live a life honorable to God.

I went in the fall of 1687 [to Lueneburg to study exegesis] with great joy, since I hoped to achieve perfectly my chief task by doing so, namely to become a justified Christian [He was asked to preach a sermon on John 20:31.] My mind was in such a state that I was not only concerned with the mere preaching of a sermon but chiefly with the upbuilding of the congregation. Earnestly considering this matter, the thought came to me that I did not find the faith in myself that I was to demand in the sermon. I therefore left off meditation on the sermon and found enough to meditate on in myself. The fact that I had no true belief troubled me in an ever more serious way.

I also knew what it was to see the heart's misery and great sorrow daily, and yet not know or understand any Savior or any refuge. In such great dread I went once more upon my knees on the evening before the Sunday on which I was to preach. I cried to God, whom I still did not know nor trust, for salvation from such a miserable state (asking him to save me), if indeed he was a true God. The Lord, the living God, heard my cry from his throne while I yet knelt. So great was his fatherly love that he wished to take me finally, after such doubts and unrest of my heart, so that I might be more convinced that he could satisfy me well, and that my erring reason might be tamed, so as not to move against his power and faithfulness. He immediately heard me. My doubt vanished as quickly as one turns one's hand; I was assured in my heart of the grace of God in Christ Jesus and I knew God not only as God but as my Father. All sadness and unrest of my heart was taken away at once, and I was immediately overwhelmed as with a stream of joy so that with full joy I praised and gave honor to God who has shown me such great grace. I arose a completely different person from the one who had knelt down. When I knelt down I did not believe that there was a God but when I stood up I believed it to the point of giving up my blood without fear or doubt. I then went to bed, but because of the great joy I could not sleep and if I closed my eyes for a few minutes I woke up again and began anew to praise, give honor, and acknowledge the living God who had given himself to be known by my soul.

Nevertheless, the thought came to me that this experience could be natural, that one could also experience such great joy naturally, but I was completely and totally convinced that this was not false and that all the world with all its joy and glory could not awaken such sweetness in the human heart as the sweetness I had, and I saw in faith that after such a foretaste of grace and the goodness of God, the world with its attractions to worldly joys would have little more hold on me. The streams of the living water were so lovely for me that I could easily forget the stinking swamps of this world.[7]

We see the same complex in Franke's conversion as we saw in Augustine's. Franke experienced a profound desire to be freed from the power of sin. He made promises to reform himself, but was never able to fulfill them. He wanted to study the Bible so that he could become a "justified Christian." His use of the term shows that he was familiar with it. Within the Lutheran religious context in which he had been raised, that term was used as Luther and the Scriptures use it.

Franke must have heard that justification came by faith in Christ's work on the cross. But he uses the term in the way Augustine used it. He wanted to become just in his actions. Moreover, his conversion was not effected by the message of forgiveness. It came through an act of God directly on his heart. The assurance of his conversion rested not on Christ's forgiveness, but on his opinion that anything that felt so real could not be false.

Franke and the Pietistic movement were the seedbed of the early Lutheran mission work in our country that spawned the churches that make up the Evangelical Lutheran Church in America today.

---

[7]Peter Erb, ed., *Pietists, Selected Writings* (New York: Paulist Press, 1983), pp. 99ff.

John Wesley's conversion

John Wesley was the founder of the Methodist denomination. His conversion was much the same as Franke's. He, too, wanted to become more holy in his life. His conversion experience answered that desire.

> In this vile, abject state of bondage to sin, I was indeed fighting continually, but not conquering. Before, I had willingly served sin; now it was unwillingly; but still I served it. I fell, and rose, and fell again. Sometimes I was overcome, and in heaviness: Sometimes I overcame, and was in joy. For as in the former state I had some foretastes of the terrors of the law, so had I in this, of the comforts of the gospel. During this whole struggle between nature and grace, which had now continued above ten years, I had many remarkable returns to prayer; especially when I was in trouble. But I was still "under the law," not "under grace": For I was only striving with, not freed from, sin: neither had I the witness of the Spirit with my spirit, and indeed could not; for I "sought it not by faith, but as it were by the works of the law."

> [He met a man named Peter Boehler who explained "salvation by grace" to him.] "Nor could I therefore allow it to be true, till I found some living witnesses of it." He [Boehler] replied, he could show me such at any time; if I desired it, the next day. And accordingly, the next day he came again with three others, all of whom testified, of their own personal experience, that a true living faith in Christ is inseparable from a sense of pardon for all past, and freedom from all present sins. They added with one mouth, that this faith was the gift, the free gift of God; and that

he would surely bestow it upon every soul who earnestly and perseveringly sought it. I was not thoroughly convinced; and, by the grace of God, I resolved to seek it unto the end, 1. By absolutely renouncing all dependence in whole or in part, upon my own works or righteousness; on which I had really grounded my hope of salvation, though I knew it not, from my youth up; 2. By adding to the constant use of all the other means of grace, continual prayer for this very thing, justifying, saving faith, a full reliance on the blood of Christ shed for me; a trust in Him, as my Christ, as my sole justification, sanctification, and redemption.

[Shortly after that meeting with Boehler] In the evening I went very unwillingly to a society in Aldersgate-Street, where one was reading Luther's preface to the Epistle to the Romans. About a quarter before nine while he was describing the change which God works in the heart through faith in Christ, I felt my heart strangely warmed. I felt I did trust in Christ, Christ alone for salvation: And an assurance was given me, that he had taken away my sins, even mine, and saved me from the law of sin and death.[8]

In Wesley's conversion account we note the same things we noted in the others. First, and most important, there is an intense longing for morality. Second, this longing is coming from a person who already is familiar with God's Word and who knows that Christ died on the cross for his sins. Granted, Wesley states that his coming to faith meant he now knew that God had taken away his sins. Yet, he was trying to become a more

---

[8]John Wesley, *The Works of John Wesley,* vol. 1 (Kansas City: Nazarene Publishing House, n.d.), pp. 101-103.

moral person and put away the sins that were troubling him. Third, we hear that Wesley's spiritual advisors put him in the state of mind where he anticipated a searching and finding. Wesley resolved to "seek it unto the end." When he found it, he found the same experience of conversion as Augustine and Franke did.[9]

These conversion experiences shared much in common. The theology that flowed from these men also shared similarities. Their theology was consistent with the *goal of their search*—morality and its attendant blessings. Augustine shifted the meaning of justification to a "making righteous" and set the tone for subsequent Roman Catholic discussions of justification and grace, which came to mean primarily an infused quality. Franke was a chief figure in the Pietistic movement. This movement emphasized sanctification. Wesley's movement is well known in history. While it was very successful, it never went beyond a heavy emphasis on the methods of obtaining an experience of Christian perfection.[10]

---

[9]It might be argued that Wesley's Aldersgate experience meant a profound change in his Christian outlook. Stanley Ayling writes, "That there is any clear boundary between Wesley's life before a quarter to nine on the evening of 24 May 1738, and his life after that point, is a proposition which accords neither with the apparent facts nor even with a good deal of Wesley's own subsequent testimony, however lovingly he might sometimes luxuriate in this legend himself." Stanley Ayling, *John Wesley* (New York: William Collins, 1979), p. 93. This is not to say that Luther had no influence over Wesley. He helped him to understand "by faith alone" and Wesley would repeat Luther's words often. But the basic struggle of Wesley to become more moral would continue, and to say that justification played the central role in his attaining that sanctification would be saying too much. His subsequent life showed that he was far from Lutheran, and his pre-Aldersgate search for the moral life was still at the center of his theology.

[10]For an excellent discussion of Christian perfection see Charles W. Carter, *A Contemporary Wesleyan Theology,* vol. 2 (Grand Rapids: Zondervan, 1983), pp. 521-565. In this section he states that "perfection" does not mean being perfect, but rather experiencing the second blessing that impels a man forward toward the goal of perfection.

When we compare Calvin with these men, we find similarities. In spite of all the good things Calvin had to say about justification, his emphasis was shifted in the same direction as theirs. He wanted to become more moral. He says little about his conversion, but refers to it in the preface to his *Commentary on the Psalms:* "First, when I was too firmly addicted to the papal superstitions to be drawn easily out of such a deep mire, by a sudden conversion He brought my mind (already more rigid than suited my age) to submission to him."[11]

Saint Paul uses the term "submission" in Romans 10:3 ("they did not submit to God's righteousness") to refer to submitting by faith to God's righteousness as a gift. Calvin had in mind a moral submission, as his understanding of the gospel and the kingdom of God shows. Much of his *Institutes* refers to the new life of service to God, and the history of his moral reforms in Geneva indicates that he drifted in the direction of "becoming righteous," rather than wanting to know that God had declared him righteous.

I agree with McGrath's statement about the Swiss Reformation: "As will become clear in the present study, the origins of the Reformed church owe little, if anything, to Luther's insights into justification."[12] This was because Calvin did not go beyond Augustine in his essential understanding of justification. For him the emphasis was on a moral change.

John Bunyan's conversion

John Bunyan's conversion shows that all of this is not simply a neat division along denominational lines. Bunyan (1628-1688) was born and grew up in Puritan England. As such, he was brought up in a religious environ-

---

[11]Hugh T. Kerr and John M. Mulder, eds., *Conversions* (Grand Rapids: Eerdmans, 1983), p. 25.

[12]McGrath, *Iustitia Dei,* vol. 2, p. 1.

ment. Yet he confesses he was a real sinner in his youth—so much so, that he feared he had given up any chance of finding favor with God.

This desire—namely, to find favor with God—is refreshing in his conversion account. He does not dwell on the desire to put off the sins of the flesh, as the others had done. Rather, he sought peace with an angry God.

The following excerpt from *Grace Abounding To The Chief Of Sinners* depicts Bunyan expressing his doubt about whether God would ever receive him back into his favor. At first, he hopes that God will return with his favor "after many days," that is, that God will not desert him eternally. He continues to study the Bible and comes across the phrase, "my grace is sufficient." Still, he finds no comfort until he focuses on the next two words of the phrase, "for thee." That gives him hope. But Satan reminds him of how Esau was rejected by his father, who would not give him the birthright even though he pleaded for it with tears. Bunyan describes how he went back and forth between hope and doubt.

> Thus I went on for many weeks, sometimes comforted, and sometimes tormented; and especially at some times my torment would be very sore. . . .
>
> But one day, as I was passing into the field, and that too with some dashes on my conscience, fearing lest yet all was not right, suddenly this sentence fell upon my soul, "Thy righteousness is in heaven;" and methought withal, I saw with the eyes of my soul, Jesus Christ at God's right hand; there, I say, as my righteousness; so that wherever I was, or whatever I was doing, God could not say to me, "He wants my righteousness," for that was just before him. I also saw moreover, that it was not my good frame of heart that made my righteousness better, nor yet my

bad frame that made my righteousness worse; for my righteousness was Jesus Christ himself, "the same yesterday, today and for ever."

Now did my chains fall off my legs indeed; I was loosed from my afflictions and irons; my temptations also fled away; so that from that time those dreadful Scriptures of God [i.e. concerning Esau's rejection] left off to trouble me: now went I also home rejoicing, for the grace and love of God; so when I came home, I looked to see if I could find that sentence, "Thy righteousness is in heaven," but could not find such a saying; wherefore my heart began to sink again, only that was brought to my remembrance, "He is made unto us of God, wisdom, righteousness, sanctification, and redemption." By this word I saw the other sentence true.

For by this Scripture I saw that the man Christ Jesus, as he is distinct from us, as touching his bodily presence, so he is our righteousness and sanctification before God. Here therefore I lived, for some time, very sweetly at peace with God through Christ. Oh! methought, Christ! Christ! there was nothing but Christ that was before my eyes. . . . Now Christ was all; all my righteousness, all my sanctification, and all my redemption.

Further, the Lord did also lead me into the mystery of the union with the Son of God, that I was joined to him, and that I was flesh of his flesh, and bone of his bone, and now was that a sweet word unto me, in Ephes. v. 30. By this also was my faith in him, as my righteousness, the more confirmed in me; for if he and I were one, then his righteousness was mine, his merits mine, his victory also mine.[13]

---

[13]Kerr and Mulder, *Conversions,* pp. 52,53.

These are wonderful words by Bunyan. While they might not have filtered down into his entire system of beliefs, they show a man who like Luther was focusing on finding peace with God, and who found it in the objective words of Scripture.

Martin Luther's conversion

Martin Luther did not dwell on his conversion. This was not because he did not experience a dramatic change. Rather, it was because he came to understand that the nature of justification was the same as his conversion. Roland Bainton quotes Luther, as the reformer describes his conversion,

> Is it not against all natural reason that God out of his mere whim deserts men, hardens them, damns them, as if he delighted in sins and in such torments of the wretched for eternity, he who is said to be of such mercy and goodness? This appears iniquitous, cruel, and intolerable in God, by which very many have been offended in all ages. And who would not be? I was myself more than once driven to the very abyss of despair so that I wished I had never been created.[14]

> I greatly longed to understand Paul's Epistle to the Romans and nothing stood in the way but that one expression, "the justice of God," because I took it to mean that justice whereby God is just and deals justly in punishing the unjust. My situation was that, although an impeccable monk, I stood before God as a sinner troubled in conscience, and I had no confidence that my merit

---

[14]Roland Bainton, *Here I Stand* (Nashville: Abingdon, 1950), p. 59.

would assuage him. Therefore I did not love a just and angry God, but rather hated and murmured against him. Yet I clung to the dear Paul and had a great yearning to know what he meant.

Night and day I pondered until I saw the connection between the justice of God and the statement that "the just shall live by his faith." Then I grasped that the justice of God is that righteousness by which through grace and sheer mercy God justifies us through faith. Thereupon I felt myself to be reborn and to have gone through open doors into paradise. The whole of Scripture took on a new meaning, and whereas before the "justice of God" had filled me with hate, now it became to me inexpressibly sweet in greater love. This passage of Paul became to me a gate to heaven.[15]

In one of his hymns, Luther describes his conversion:

> Fast bound in Satan's chains I lay,
> Death brooded darkly o'er me,
> Sin was my torment night and day,
> In sin my mother bore me;
> Yea, deep and deeper still I fell,
> Life had become a living hell,
> So firmly sin possessed me.
>
> He spoke to his beloved Son:
> 'Tis time to have compassion.
> Then go, bright Jewel of My crown,
> And bring to man salvation;
> From sin and sorrow set him free,
> Slay bitter death for him that he
> May live with Thee forever.

---

[15]Ibid., p. 66.

> To me he spake: Hold Fast to me,
> I am thy Rock and Castle;
> Thy Ransom I Myself will be,
> For thee I strive and wrestle;
> For I am with thee, I am thine,
> And evermore thou shalt be Mine;
> The Foe shall not divide us.[16]

We sense a difference in Luther. He was not trying to become a better person by coming to faith. He realized he was a sinner, and there was nothing he could do to become sanctified enough to be acceptable to God.

Martin Luther's conversion was a discovery of an objective truth. He came to understand that God had prepared a righteousness for him in Christ. His faith and his conversion were centered on a fact. It was an answer to the terror of standing in front of God and having only the law with its curse standing there with him. The answer Luther found impelled him forward in the work of reforming the church and leading others to the peace he had found.

This chapter was not included to lead us to doubt our individual conversions or to suggest that the Holy Spirit did not work with the law and the gospel in the hearts of the first three men we have considered. We do not question the genuineness of the faith of men like Augustine and the others, since trusting in God's forgiveness was in fact a part of spiritual life. Rather, it was included to help us sense the two basic conversion experiences, so that we tailor our methods to effect a conversion in line with God's Word where guilt and forgiveness are *central* to the faith that results. Such a conversion truly leads to peace with God.

---

[16]*The Lutheran Hymnal* (Saint Louis: Concordia, 1941), Hymn 387. This was Luther's first congregational hymn, written in 1523.

7.

THE LUTHERAN UNDERSTANDING
OF GRACE

The Biblical/Lutheran paradox regarding grace

The gospel of justification will be our point of reference as we examine Church Growth methods. The question some might be asking is, "Why is understanding this distinction between the Lutheran and the Evangelical/Reformed theology so important? Can't both exist side by side? Doesn't each theology have its strong points and weak points?"

A brief digression into the Lutheran understanding of the fact of "by grace alone," will help us arrive at an answer to that question and see how vital it is to understand the distinction we have been working on.

Lutheran theology, based on Scripture, maintains that people are without any ability to come to faith. It is solely by the grace of God that we are enabled to be contrite and to believe that the crucified and risen Jesus is our Savior from the guilt and punishment of sin.

Much of the history of the Lutheran church has centered on this truth. One of Martin Luther's most important books, *The Bondage of the Will,* was written against Erasmus's teachings about the freedom of the human will to carry out God's commands. Shortly after Luther's death, Philip Melanchthon, Luther's closest co-worker, began to teach that people have the natural ability to apply themselves to receiving God's grace. His statements to this effect caused the Lutheran church of his day to divide. The greatest American intra-Lutheran doctrinal conflict took place over the teaching of election and the accompanying teaching about the meaning of "grace alone."

Following the Bible and the Lutheran confessions, Lutherans have taught that God's grace does absolutely everything for our salvation. God's grace began with his electing the Christian from eternity to come to faith; it continued with God's calling and forgiving him; it will remain until the end of time when God glorifies him. (See Romans 8:29,30.) There is no room for man's aid or cooperation in contributing something toward his salvation, either by way of works or by way of some natural inclination to come to faith. (See Romans 3:10,11; 8:6,7.)

Lutherans take the glorious song of praise of Ephesians 1 at face value. From beginning to end, God's grace has brought us to where we are as Christians.

In addition to rejecting our own powers in coming to faith, we believe that if a person rejects God's grace, the fault lies completely with that person and not with God (Matthew 23:37,38). Lutherans also reject the error of Calvin who limited the scope of God's salvation. Indeed, God wants all people to be saved (1 Timothy 2:4).

These beliefs create a paradox. They cannot both be embraced simultaneously by sinful human logic. According to our logic, there has to be a difference either in (1) how people use their power of "free choice" or (2) how God deals with people. But faith accepts both "conflicting" truths of salvation by grace alone, and God's intent that all be saved (in the face of the fact that all are not).

Logically, this paradox does not make sense, but theologically, and in every Christian's day by day experience, it fits his understanding of conversion and justification. First, the Christian who has experienced God's law working on his heart to reveal to him the punishment he deserves, and then comes to know Christ's forgiveness, knows that he did not choose God, but that God, in his grace, chose him to know his sins and to come to faith in Christ's forgiveness. He also trusts that God will preserve him in faith. This is his confidence. Second, the Christian does not for this reason become sinfully secure, for he knows he would fall if he became proud and forgot about the guilt of his sins and did not depend on God's forgiveness to sustain him. On both fronts the Christian is led to God's grace and pardon to sustain him, for paradoxically he knows that his sinful nature would reject God's grace at the first opportunity.

Lutherans have realized from Scripture that the teaching of "by grace alone" must stand secure or Christianity will fall. If the door is left open to our efforts or works, we are back under the dominion of the law (Romans 4:14,15). The paradox, which is part of the teaching of grace, must remain intact also. To doubt God's will for me, or to rely on my own strength to contribute to my faith, will ultimately lead me away from God.

The importance of the paradox

We can now attempt to look at the whole picture and see why the distinctions we have been making are so important for our Christianity.

Why do Calvinists and particularly Arminians (and, for that matter, Romans Catholics) reject the paradox? Is it because they cannot understand the words of Scripture? Is it because they are less astute than Lutherans? The answer to both questions is no. The reason they reject Scripture's emphasis on "by grace alone" is that their initial focus prior to their "conversion," their conversion itself, and their subsequent Christian focus lead them away from grace and ultimately from the gospel. How and why does it do this?

Simply put, whenever anyone shifts his focus of Christianity, as the Evangelical/Reformed do, his "faith" is no longer a miracle the Holy Spirit works through the gospel. We must realize that there is in man a natural desire to want to keep the law. While most consider this desire to be an example of the innate goodness of man, or the "prevenient grace" of the Holy Spirit, the Bible tells us that in the true spiritual sense, no one yearns for the law or for the true spiritual means of fulfilling it in their lives. (See Romans 3:10,11; 8:6,7.)

What, then, is this yearning that so many experience? Lutherans have called this the *opinio legis,* or the natural (and sinful) desire of a person to gain something for himself by keeping the law, whether that happens to be heaven or God's temporal blessings on earth. We hold that even the desire to be moral is a sin—unless that morality is fostered by a love for the Lord. But such a love can only come when a person first knows that God has loved and forgiven him. The *opinio legis* often exhibits itself in the most pious way. Often it's accompanied by a fine sounding confession that God alone must finally give one the answer to his request. To be sure, often God uses this desire in beneficial ways, for the welfare of mankind and to keep order in society. He blesses those who do what they know is morally right. But ultimately, the spirit that yearns for this morality, for a reason other than to thank God for his forgiveness, is either a human spirit or a supernatural one that does not come from God.

By focusing their religion on the positive effects of keeping the law, the Evangelicals are working with something the human spirit *can* muster by its own strength. They are working with a natural spirit, and their religion ultimately will gravitate toward an emphasis on the law to sustain the spirit they received in their conversion.

How does this tie in with the paradox of grace? When Evangelical/Reformed people destroy this paradox, they are giving witness to the fact that the spirit they are working with is a human spirit—the spirit of the *opinio legis*. They are saying that their experience in gaining or keeping this spirit has not demonstrated to them that it came by the grace of God alone. Rather, it originated at least in part from their own spiritual powers.

It's not that the Evangelical wants to turn salvation into works. What happens, however, is that his initial starting point of yearning for moral improvement has already moved his understanding of Christianity into the area of human ethical action. To the extent that one's Christianity focuses on this, he is working with another spirit, a spirit he *can* effect through what he does.

To make a decision and to be filled with the Reformed spirit—the "I found it" claim—is indeed something that people can do by their own power. Such a decision issues from man's natural desire to become more moral. What I am saying is that one *can* make a decision to turn one's life over to serving God's laws. But one *cannot* make a decision to be born into God's household through hearing of the gospel of forgiveness in Christ (John 1:12,13).

Breaking the paradox, then, is more a symptom of what has happened in a person's heart at conversion than an understandable misinterpreting of Scripture. To the extent we Lutherans have incorporated a spirit of deadness, or of serving the sinful nature, we deserve to be rebuked. But the answer to that problem must never be a yearning for the Evangelical/Reformed spirit of morality. What we need is a renewed emphasis on the law and the gospel.

Robbed of the gospel

The Evangelical/Reformed theological and experiential complex tragically robs people of the hope the real gospel brings. Breaking the paradox places a person outside of grace, and under the law. Once under the law, if a person is consistent with his stand, he has fallen from grace. To him, the gospel ceases to be the good news of God's complete forgiveness in Christ; it becomes a power that has only partially done its work of making the person's life free of sin and its affects.

When we look for empirical results of this "gospel," we invariably lose hope in it. The kingdom of God becomes less than the perfect peace we have through God's pardon. Instead, it becomes only partially in effect, as evidenced by the sin and suffering in the world and in our lives. When this happens, we cannot but lose hope in the security of such a kingdom.

The Evangelical/Reformed spirit lives outside of the Lutheran paradox doctrinally. The second part of our book will seek to demonstrate that this spirit remains methodologically outside the paradox as well. The Lutheran spirit remains within this paradox doctrinally, and must do so methodologically. Any program or theory the Lutheran church develops that breaks this paradox will inevitably lead into the Evangelical/Reformed camp and its pitfalls.

This link between the nature of the gospel and the paradox of grace will help us later, when we discuss two Church Growth concepts—the desire to grow and Church Growth's use of visions and goals. We get to that in chapters 10 and 11.

8.

TWO DIFFERENT SPIRITS

When we deal with Lutheran and Reformed theology, we are actually dealing with two different spirits. The contrasts in doctrine and the conversion experience are so basically different that they can only come from two different spirits. Luther saw this clearly. And I believe that the Evangelical/Reformed would accept this statement also, only differing with Lutherans on who has the true spirit.

We can now attempt to summarize the distinction between Lutheran and Reformed theology by drawing some contrasts. What follows is only a brief sketch and one can easily add other contrasts to the list.

A brief catalog of differences

Reformed theology says that where there is life and salvation, there is also the forgiveness of sins. Lutheran theology says that where there is the forgiveness of sins, there is also life and salvation.

Reformed theology stems from the struggle of a sinner to become sanctified. Lutheran theology stems from the relief a sinner feels when he knows that God has justified him in Christ.

Reformed theology views sin "primarily as a weakness or lack of potential happiness." Lutherans view sin as "rebellion against God . . . which causes God to be consumed with wrath."[1]

Reformed theology stems from the struggle a person has in achieving the kind of faith that will make a moral transformation possible. Reformed theology, therefore, considers the law as a means toward accomplishing the goal of conversion by driving a person to make a moral choice for God. Lutheran theology, on the other hand, considers the law's role in conversion to be the tool God uses to make a person realize he cannot measure up even if he would make a moral commitment to God.

In Reformed theology the law has been given primarily to make a person happy. In Lutheran theology the law has been given primarily to make a person miserable; happiness comes later as the believer finds joy in serving his Savior.

In Reformed theology, a person's preparation for the gospel is a process of realizing the effects of sin that lead him to want to amend his ways and serve God. In Lutheran theology, the effect of the law is sorrow over the guilt of sin that, unless the gospel intervenes, only drives a person further from God and makes him more rebellious than he was before.

In Reformed theology, obedience becomes integrated with faith. Faith is viewed as an act through which a

---

[1]Klemet Preus, "Contemporary Christian Music: An Evaluation," *Concordia Theological Quarterly,* 51, (January 1987?), p. 13.

person fulfills the conditions necessary to receive an infusion of power by being united with Christ. Lutheran theology stems from faith in a fact. Faith is viewed only as the hand that receives the forgiveness Christ has won for the world. In Lutheran theology, faith is kept separate from our obedience, for the object of our faith is Christ's obedience.

Reformed theology centers on the Word of God because it expresses God's will for life. Lutheran theology centers on the Word because the Word contains the message of forgiveness in Christ.[2]

Reformed theology weights the concept of salvation in the direction of deliverance from the power of sin (although deliverance from the guilt of sin is also a major theme). Lutheran theology weights the concept of salvation in the direction of deliverance from the guilt of sin (which in turn leads to deliverance from the power of sin).

Reformed theology leads to an emphasis on a distinct experience of an infusion of the Spirit. Experience in Lutheran theology flows from the Spirit's leading a person to know he is justified.

Reformed theology does not consider the Word to be the means of grace as Lutheran theology does. When the focus is on sanctification, the Word becomes a source of instruction to be used by the Spirit who comes at conversion (either through God's sovereign choice or through man's decision). Lutheran theology considers the Word of God to be the means of grace in the sense that it alone reveals God's gracious forgiveness. God's grace comes to a person through the Word, and the Spirit uses that Word to create faith in his heart.

Reformed theology considers baptism to be a sign of something already done in man's heart. Here we see

---

[2]See Hermann Sasse, *Here We Stand,* trans. Theodore Tappert (Saint Louis: Concordia, 1966), pp. 57ff.

clearly the result of the Evangelical conversion experience. Children simply cannot have that sort of experience. The accompanying Evangelical teaching of the "age of accountability" fits into the picture also. A desire for morality can only be made when a child has developed an awareness necessary to make such a decision. Lutheran theology considers baptism the means by which God brings a child the forgiveness of sins. Nothing else is required for this act than a subject who is sinful.

Reformed theology considers the Lord's Supper to be less than a sacrament. Its emphasis on a decision for morality undermines an appreciation of Scripture that should lead believers to treasure the body and blood of Christ as the means by which God gives us forgiveness. This is what Lutherans do.

Reformed theology is a theology of glory, in the sense that its spirit promises and effects empirical results that a person can rejoice in. Lutheran theology is the theology of the cross, in the sense that we glory in the cross and live by faith—a faith that is begun and kept alive by God's absolution of our sins.[3]

Reformed theology must consider our present situation to be an "in between time" when the full force of Christ's victory and the establishment of the kingdom of God has yet to be experienced by the church. Lutheran theology knows that God's kingdom is in full force, guiding all things for the good of the growth and maintenance of God's church, even though the evidence most often points to the contrary.

Since its focus is on the empirical results of the kingdom of God, Reformed theology tends toward an earthly

---

[3]See Harold L. Senkbeil, *Sanctification: Christ in Action* (Milwaukee: Northwestern Publishing House, 1989). Senkbeil contrasts the emphasis on the empirical "life-style" result in Evangelical Christianity with the Lutheran focus on God's forgiveness.

millennial hope of one sort or another. Lutheran theology looks forward to a new heaven and earth, the home of righteousness.

Finally, since people by nature long for morality and order, Reformed theology tends toward a higher view of the power of man's will. It considers this natural longing to be God's prevenient grace, working to lead people to seek morality. This seeking hopefully will lead them to find God and submit to him in conversion. Lutheran theology states that while man might desire morality, no person is able to desire Christian conversion, properly understood, for conversion means setting aside our own moral agenda and coming before God as those who have sinned, wanting not morality but forgiveness. Only the Spirit of God can effect such a desire. While Reformed evangelism can tap into the natural desires, Lutheran evangelism cannot.

The gospel and . . .

Reformed theology presents an incomplete gospel, since the gospel is viewed as the good news that God will renew a person—and renewal is never complete. Lutheran theology presents a complete gospel, since Christ's forgiveness is indeed complete.

Reformed theology presents an incomplete kingdom of God, since the reality of the kingdom is measured in the observable results of God's rule. Lutheran theology presents a completed kingdom in as much as God's rule over Satan is completely established through Jesus' victory on the cross.

Reformed theology presents an incomplete conversion since conversion is viewed as a turning from wrong to right—and such a turning is never complete this side of heaven. Lutheran theology presents a conversion in which there is confidence, since conversion is turning to a Savior whose work on our behalf is completely finished.

Reformed theology presents a teaching of partial grace, since man's self determination enters into the conversion equation. Lutheran theology presents a teaching of pure grace and the comfort it brings. Lutheran theology is content to live with the paradox that grace presents.

A picture will help us summarize the root of the issue. There is a picture that Protestant Christians—both Reformed and Lutherans—like to use to express the relation between justification and sanctification. The picture is of an engine pulling a train. The engine is justification which, as it's explained, always comes first. The cars, which represent sanctification, always follow behind, just as sanctification follows justification.

This picture fits much better with Reformed theology than it does with Lutheran theology. The purpose of a train is to pull the cars. The chief objects of attention are the cars. The engine is a tool for pulling the cars. It is valuable only because it pulls the cars. If there are no cars following, the engine is not considered really to be "doing" anything.

While this picture describes a certain relationship, it does not describe the position the Lutheran Church gives to the gospel. It describes the Reformed position that to a greater or lesser extent looks at the gospel as a tool to be used for sanctification. As a mere tool, it does not achieve center stage.

Lutherans are happy because they have an engine. They focus on it, for it will take them to eternal life. More and more cars will be added to the train. Every one that is added will cause the Christian to praise God. Yet even without any cars, the engine is God's power for salvation.

Understanding and truly appreciating the gospel involves more than understanding the relationship between faith and works, between justification and sanctification. In order truly to understand and appreciate the gospel, there has to be an emptiness that only forgiveness can fill. When there is a desire for forgiveness it is difficult to misunderstand the gospel as being an infusion of virtue.

When it is taught that the gospel is the forgiveness of sins, sanctification falls into place. The life and works of a Christian are his response to the treasure he has discovered. When a person openly or secretly desires morality and its blessings, the gospel becomes merely a tool. It becomes something to be used. In the process, sanctification becomes something one does because of the benefits he accrues and not because he is trying to bring the cars of his life into line with the path of the engine.

In a religious climate in which heaven and hell are held before the people, as in the church of Martin Luther's day, Christianity becomes a religion of open work righteousness with the goal being eternal life. To a great extent in our modern world, people live in a climate of secularized religion. Thoughts of heaven and hell are not immediate. As a result, they look primarily for what Christianity can give them to help them in their lives, to enable them to get through another day, and for a philosophy to help them make sense of the world.

Only when faith is conceived of as the hand that receives the gifts of forgiveness can there be any real guarantee of salvation. Only when the goal of Christianity becomes the forgiveness of sins will eternity or life now become sure, for only within that context can life be lived not by sight, but by faith in a God whose love in all things is guaranteed. Only then can we live by the Spirit and produce his fruits.

Before we proceed, we need to reemphasize one more qualification. The shift in emphasis we have been trying to describe is not something one finds in its pure form on either end of the continuum. There are many in the Reformed churches that understand grace and forgiveness better than many Lutherans. There are Lutherans who view their religion as primarily a way to become more moral.

The diagram below illustrates this continuum. On the left are those who are totally committed to this world. They understand the gospel and the kingdom as the results of God's rule on this earth. On the right are those who understand that the center of Christianity is the forgiveness of sins that God effected through his Son's death and resurrection. Between the ends of the continuum are many mixtures and variations. I also believe that no one is completely free from trying to "use" God to help him in bettering his life here and now.

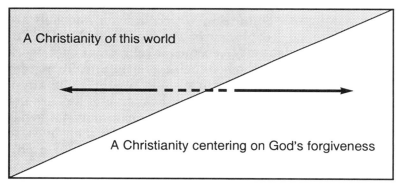

A Christianity of this world

A Christianity centering on God's forgiveness

Conclusion

This chapter has reviewed the basic theological contrasts we must keep in mind as we develop methodology. Looking ahead, some of the questions we will ask are: Is a particular method conducive to fostering a real sense of sin and guilt before God? Does it lead a person to know Christ's forgiveness as his greatest treasure? Or does it lead to a desire for morality? Does it undermine the "paradox" of Scripture that must be maintained if true Christianity is to continue? Or does it uphold this paradox and work within its tension?

These are questions Lutherans must ask of methods in general, and of Church Growth methods in particular.

Part Two:

THEOLOGY AND THEORY IN THE CHURCH GROWTH MOVEMENT AND IN LUTHERAN MINISTRY

INTRODUCTION TO PART TWO

We turn now from theology to methodology. The purpose of this part of the book is to show why Church Growth methods fit perfectly with Reformed theology, but not with Lutheran theology as we have defined it. We'll consider how methods flow from a particular theological standpoint and why they do so. (It might be helpful to recall the diagram on page xi.)

If the Reformed understanding of the gospel as infused grace is correct, then the Church Growth movement must serve as our paradigm for ministry. It is indeed an embodiment of that theology. If the gospel is God's forgiveness, however, then many Church Growth methods will not serve our purposes.

We need to make two points before we continue. First, methods are not neutral. The assertion that they are is made only by (1) people who are trying to make a shift in the practice of ministry and do not wish to deal with the theological implications of their actions, (2) people who share an understanding of the gospel with those whose methods they want to use, or (3) people who are thinking of basic methods in an abstract way, such as "preaching," "canvassing," or "advertising," and have not fleshed out these abstractions to the point where they can actually be put to use.

Second, Church Growth is a movement that is too broad to cover in any one book or by any one person, except perhaps by a few who are in leadership positions in the movement. It encompasses theory and methodology in both foreign and domestic missions. In the sphere of domestic missions, it deals with large congregations, small congregations, and especially the planting of new congregations.

In the next chapter I will give a brief historical and theological sketch of the Church Growth movement. Succeeding chapters in Part Two will discuss what I consider to be basic issues raised by Church Growth that pertain to outreach mindsets and methods for American congregations.

9.

THE WORLD OF CHURCH GROWTH

Just what is Church Growth? The phrase "Church Growth Movement" might seem to denote something specific. Yet taking away the capital letters, "church growth movement" would seem to denote something rather nebulous, a movement that probably wouldn't be associated with any single person or principle. In fact, the Church Growth Movement is both specific and general. This paradox is something the movement itself lives with. One analyst writes:

Like any idea whose time has come it is not easy to pin down. Church growth, simple as it may seem, is in fact a diffuse and varied concept. It can mean different things to different people. It can be expressed in very different ways and be found in many different forms. For some the meaning is clear and obvious, containing within it a known package of theological and ecclesiological assumptions. "Church Growth" becomes a rallying call to fall in behind a particular movement with its esoteric vocabulary and mode of working. For others, interest is more eclectic and general, a willingness to draw up any or all who seem to be able to illuminate the present situation, who can provide ways and means in a task.[1]

Which meaning, the specific or the general, suits the Church Growth Movement today? I would say both. The movement still tries to maintain an identity that centers on some basic ideas that are either unique or very important to the movement. Yet, the movement is also quite eclectic as any Church Growth bibliography will show.

Background of the movement

The Church Growth Movement grew out of the struggles of a foreign missionary named Donald McGavran. McGavran was a third generation missionary working in India for the Disciples of Christ and had become overseer of their mission by the mid 1930s. His frustration began building when he saw that none of the seventeen churches under his care was growing, and that during the mission's fifty years of work only 2000 had been converted. For some time prior to his leaving the mission in 1954, McGavran had been growing in the conviction that God wanted more growth and that it would come only if mission work was done in an "enlightened" way. McGavran wrote:

---

[1]Paul Ballard, "The Question of Church Growth," *The Baptist Quarterly* (October 1980), p. 361.

A vast curiosity was born within me. What *does* make churches grow? More importantly, what makes many churches *stop* growing? How is it possible for Christians to come out of ripe harvest fields empty-handed? Answering the question— what are the *causes* of church growth, and what are the *obstacles* to church growth became the chief purpose of my life.[2]

What grew out of McGavran's frustrations became the Church Growth Movement. Up until the early 1970s, McGavran's work centered in foreign missions. He continually worked to develop his ideas and hypotheses. His journey led him to Fuller Theological Seminary, Pasadena, California, where he established the School of World Missions. That school has become the think tank of the Church Growth Movement.

The conscious effort to apply Church Growth thinking to America was stimulated by Pastor Charles Miller, a staff member of Pasadena's Lake Avenue Congregational Church. In 1972, he asked a member of his church, C. Peter Wagner, who was teaching with McGavran at Fuller, to organize a course for local pastors applying Church Growth principles to American churches.

Wagner and McGavran co-taught the course, and what started out as an experiment, led to a whole new movement that could be called "The American Church Growth Movement." One man who attended that first class in 1972, Win Arn, is today the leading promoter of Church Growth ideas in America. His Institute for American Church Growth produces films and seminars that reach all areas of North America.

The movement has expanded throughout the Evangelical world. Some organizations are direct spinoffs of the

---

[2]Donald McGavran and George Hunger, *Church Growth: Strategies That Work* (Nashville: Abingdon, 1960), p. 16.

Fuller School of World Missions. The Charles E. Fuller Institute of Evangelism and Church Growth is an organization associated with Fuller Seminary to provide American churches with Church Growth expertise through consultation and seminars. Various leaders have begun similar Church Growth service groups in their own denominations, such as Missouri Synod Lutheran Kent Hunter's "Church Growth Center" in Corunna, Indiana.

The principles of American Church Growth

We must realize that Church Growth is a movement. As such, it contains elements that go beyond the sum of its programs and methods. The movement is based on the numerical growth of the church. Its overriding principle is that God wants his church to grow.

Coupled with this principle is a strictly pragmatic approach to evangelism.[3] This pragmatic attitude has led McGavran and other Church Growth thinkers to assemble a list of "Church Growth Principles" defined as "a universal truth which, when properly interpreted and applied, contributes significantly to the growth of churches and denominations."[4] The Church Growth Movement's development has largely centered on "discovering" and teaching these principles.[5]

The pragmatic approach to discovering why some churches grow and others do not has led Church Growth researchers into various areas of study. As they discover the principles that make for optimum growth

---

[3]McGavran defines evangelism as, "to proclaim Jesus Christ as God and Savior, to persuade people to become his disciples and responsible members of his church." Donald A. McGavran and Win Arn, *Ten Steps for Church Growth* (San Francisco: Harper and Row, 1977), p. 51.

[4]Ibid., p. 15.

[5]C. Peter Wagner, *Your Church Can Grow* (Ventura, Calif.: Regal Books, 1976), p. 29.

in the church, they add to the mindset called "Church Growth eyes." McGavran defines this term as "a characteristic of Christians who have achieved an ability to see the possibilities for growth, and to apply appropriate strategies to gain maximum results for Christ and His Church."[6]

Developing Church Growth principles and acquiring Church Growth eyes leads one into various fields of study. Primarily, study must begin where the church is growing. In foreign missions, and to a lesser extent in the American context, "One observes where the church is growing, where God is blessing the efforts of his servants with factual, actual church growth, where the number of members is increasing and new congregations are being born."[7]

The approach to studying such growing denominations or individual congregations is by "astute observation."[8] Keeping statistics and struggling to interpret them is essential. In line with this approach is reliance on secular sociology. Since churches grow in society, an understanding of societal influences is essential for understanding growth.[9] The desire to discover church Growth principles has led Church Growth to consider itself a science. While there is an acknowledgement that the Holy Spirit is the final answer to why the church grows, the emphasis in Church Growth is to discover how he is doing it, so that Christians can take a more active role in working along with him.[10]

---

[6]McGavran and Arn, *Ten Steps,* p. 127.

[7]Ibid., pp. 15,16.

[8]Ibid., p. 17.

[9]Donald A. McGavran, *Understanding Church Growth* (Grand Rapids: Eerdmans, 1980), p. vii. It should be noted that this statement comes from the revised edition of Understanding Church Growth which reflects McGavran's later thinking.

[10]Wagner, *Your Church Can Grow,* p. 29.

The desire to discover Church Growth principles has led to many areas of study. A list of class discussion topics for Doctor of Ministry students who attend Church Growth I and II sessions at Fuller will show the range of their work.[11] Topics include Church Growth Eyes, Basic Axioms for Church Growth, Church Pathology, a listing of spiritual and sociological "diseases" that hinder or stop growth in a congregation, a listing of Spiritual Gifts and suggestions for fostering their use in the congregation, Outreach and "Body" Evangelism, statistical charting of growth patterns, understanding cultural factors, and using the homogeneous unit principle, church structuring conducive to growth, how to conduct a diagnostic test for a congregation, the profile of a "Church Growth" pastor, the role of parachurch agencies in Church Growth, new church planting—including information on site selection and urban church growth—the cell concept and how to move beyond the "single cell," helping the small church grow, church leadership, planning through visions and goals, successful "change agent" patterns, pastoring a growing church, and the value of a "signs and wonders" ministry for the growth of the church.

Obviously, the scope of Church Growth teaching is broad. The list above only includes the applications of Church Growth principles to American congregations.[12] Our study will only touch on basic issues, and the reader should be aware that there is a much larger world of Church Growth methods than we will cover here.

The theology of the Church Growth Movement

In Part One we formed a broad overview of Reformed Theology and stated that at its root it centers on the de-

---

[11]Class Notes for Church Growth I and II, Fuller Theological Seminary (1987).

[12]For an excellent overview of the Church Growth field, see C. Peter Wagner, ed. *Church Growth: State of the Art* (Wheaton, Ill.: Tyndale, 1986).

sire to become holy rather than on God's forgiveness of sins. We quoted a few church growth authors at that time. Now we will expand on the theology of Church Growth.

Some have accused the Church Growth Movement of being untheological. James Scherer writes, "Church Growth thinking is handicapped by Dr. McGavran's failure at this point to provide larger and more satisfying answers regarding the nature of the Gospel, the Church, and the Kingdom."[13]

That statement was made in 1971. I think it holds true today as well. While McGavran has studied mission work and analyzed the growth of the church throughout the world, he does not sound a very clear theological signal. Nor does Peter Wagner. The very setting of the Church Growth Movement at the multi-denominational Fuller Seminary would seem to make it rather difficult to construct a solid theological foundation on which to build strategy. Even Dr. Eddie Gibbs, who taught the "Theology of Church Growth" class at Fuller Seminary, did not tackle difficult issues, but confined his lectures to establishing biblical paradigms that supported the Church Growth emphasis.[14]

Yet, to say that the Church Growth Movement is not built on a theological foundation is incorrect. Church Growth rests solidly in the Evangelical/Reformed camp. While it does not address theological issues as it might, it nonetheless is built squarely on the Evangelical/Reformed theological complex we have discussed in Part One.

To be more specific, the Church Growth Movement fits into what is called the neo-Evangelical camp. Theologi-

---

[13]James Scherer, "The Life and Growth of Churches in Mission," IRM, LX (Jan.-Oct. 1971), p. 129, quoted in Charles Van Engen, *The Growth of the True Church* (Amsterdam: Rodopi, 1981), p. 18.

[14]For an overview of Church Growth theology, see Eddie Gibbs, *I Believe in Church Growth* (Grand Rapids: Eerdmans, 1981), pp. 15-129.

cally, this puts it in the Evangelical camp but at a certain distance from classic Evangelicalism. Richard Quebedeaux in *The Young Evangelicals* describes some of the characteristics of the Neo-Evangelicals. These characteristics also describe Fuller Seminary and the Church Growth Movement:

> First, there is emerging a fresh understanding of the reliability and authority of Scripture. The New Evangelicals are firm in their acceptance of the principle of historical criticism.
>
> Second, the New Evangelicals are again emphasizing the necessity of meaningful sanctification following regeneration. . . . There is a mounting interest among the New Evangelicals in the "social holiness" characteristic of John Wesley.
>
> Third, there is . . . a marked aversion to Dispensationalism and its inherent apocalyptic speculations [which] frees the scholars in question to deal more constructively with the present ills of society and thus develop a positive Evangelical social ethic, unhindered by . . . pessimism concerning the human condition.
>
> Fourth, [they] are displaying a fresh interest in the social dimension of the Gospel. . . . [they] hold a refreshingly optimistic theology grounded not in the innate moral possibilities within man himself but in the corporeal resurrection of Jesus Christ. . . .
>
> Fifth, the New Evangelicalism has reopened dialogue with mainstream Ecumenical Liberalism. . . .[15]

---

[15]Richard Quebedeaux, *The Young Evangelicals* (New York: Harper and Row, 1974), pp. 37-39.

Quebedeaux mentions by way of addition a sixth characteristic, "the increasing friendliness between Evangelical Christianity and science."[16]

Richard Quebedeaux's book, written over seventeen years ago, describes the present Church Growth movement's theological foundation very well. While the Church Growth movement is built on the basic foundation of Evangelical/Reformed thought—renewal and regeneration—it extends this emphasis beyond personal renewal into the need for a corporate renewal of society.

Donald McGavran began as a liberal, and has become an evangelical. In his emphasis on the growth of the church, he maintains a certain liberal flavor. On the one hand, he eschews the liberal position of mission as social service and its lack of concern about the size of the church[17]—for which he is censured by the liberals.[18] On the other hand, he maintains the view that God's work is world renewal using the church as his tool (which is a view that tends more toward a liberal standpoint). He writes:

In the last two decades of the twentieth century the Church is hearing anew God's clarion call to bring the peoples of every continent to faith and obedience. . . . It is becoming crystal clear that *there will be no great advance in righteousness, peace and justice until there are many more practicing Christians* and believing churches in every segment of mankind.

---

[16]Ibid., p. 39.

[17]Donald McGavran, *How Churches Grow* (New York: Friendship Press, 1966), pp. 68-70. (First published in the United Kingdom in 1959.)

[18]For a more liberal analysis of Church Growth, see Ralph Elliott, *Church Growth That Counts* (Valley Forge: Judson Press, 1982) and Wilbert Shenk, *Exploring Church Growth* (Grand Rapids: Eerdmans, 1983).

115

... This book is published with the prayer that it may be used of God to aid in the urgent revitalization of His Church and the incorporation of sufficient men and women in it so that major social advance may be achieved in all nations. (emphasis mine)[19]

McGavran's understudy, Peter Wagner, came into Church Growth by another route. His background is a more conservative Evangelicalism, but his emphasis is similar to McGavran's.

In *Church Growth and the Whole Gospel*, Wagner sets down his position that the gospel itself contains God's command to the church to engage in social service. He calls this the "cultural mandate." Quoting Billy Graham, he defines this simply as the command to "take regeneration in one hand and a cup of cold water in the other."[20]

We do not argue that we are to help people in their social needs. But Wagner makes this work part of the gospel itself. Wagner is speaking within the context of the Evangelical/Reformed theology that replaces the centrality of justification with the more general concept of regeneration. The gospel, which has become equivalent to regeneration (and as Wagner argues ought to become equivalent to social ministry), is no longer the free message of the forgiveness of sins. Wagner must ask, "The argument is not whether the preaching of the Gospel ought to have ethical content. . . . The question

---

[19]McGavran, *Understanding Church Growth,* p. v,vii. It should be noted that this statement comes from the revised edition of *Understanding Church Growth,* which reflects McGavran's later thinking.

[20]C. Peter Wagner, *Church Growth and the Whole Gospel* (San Francisco: Harper and Row, 1981), p. 14. The quotation is from Billy Graham, Peace with God, and was found in Arthur Johnston, *The Battle for World Evangelism* (Wheaton, Ill.: Tyndale, 1978), p. 138.

concerns the amount. How much ethical teaching is necessary for a person to be saved?"[21]

Many Evangelicals would have a hard time with that statement, as well as with the statements by McGavran quoted above. Nevertheless, these statements are logical results of the emphasis in Evangelical/Reformed circles on moral renewal. The Church Growth Movement has taken this emphasis farther than other Evangelicals who still hold to a more propositional form of Christianity, (e.g., John Calvin). The basic element of focusing on the empirical results of God's grace and power is central, and the teaching of justification as God's gift of righteousness is not.

While I cannot prove a statement like this, I can make it without any reservations. The literature of the Church Growth Movement is almost silent on the matter of God's forgiveness. In those instances where forgiveness is mentioned, it is relegated to one of the blessings of renewal, rather than the basis for it. "Knowing Christ" or "having a personal relationship with Christ" is about as far as the literature goes in defining Christianity.[22] Almost all emphasis is on the empirical results in a person's life, if he or she submits to Christ as Lord and serves him.

The only conclusion one can come to about the Church Growth Movement's understanding of the gospel is that it is the good news that God will renew his life. Anyone who reads the Lutheran understanding of the gospel into Church Growth literature is fooling himself.

---

[21]Ibid., p. 137.

[22]The definition of conversion in Wagner, *Church Growth: State of the Art*, p. 286 is, "Participation by non-Christians in a genuine decision for Christ, a sincere turning from the old gods and evil spirits, and a determined effort to live as Christ would have people live."

The above statements about the theology of Church Growth finish the work we started in Part One; they show that Church Growth theology is solidly Reformed. It will remain for us to show how Church Growth's methods flow directly out of this brand of Evangelical theology, and how they are not completely consistent with Lutheran theology. We will do this in the following chapters, as we focus on those areas of Church Growth thought that have influenced conservative Lutherans in recent years, particularly in the area of outreach and church establishment. Church Growth itself considers these issues central.

Our analysis will be built around our description of the Lutheran and scriptural understanding of the nature of the gospel. The gospel and the ministry best suited for spreading it will be our "filter" and our "fulcrum" as we carry on our analysis.

In general, each of the next chapters in this part will address the issue from four sides. First, we will state a point the Church Growth movement makes. Second, we will examine the point on the basis of Scripture. Third, we will show why the understanding of Church Growth is consistent with an Evangelical/ Reformed theological understanding of the gospel. I will also suggest how it should be viewed in the context of Lutheran theology. Finally, I will state my understanding of the issues with applications to the ministry.

Church Growth leads every pastor to deal with the following topics: (1) the desire to grow, (2) the place of visions and goals in church planning, (3) whether we should use the "felt needs" emphasis in outreach, and (4) the place of science and technology in the growth of God's church. Each of these topics is basic. They are

118

the areas with which pastors in churches such as mine must struggle.[23]

Noticeably absent from this list is a discussion of the role of the charismatic or "third wave" spirit on which C. Peter Wagner has placed greater emphasis in recent years. I have omitted this in order to confine the scope of this work. In some respects, it's one of the most important areas of study.[24]

The ensuing discussion will key off Church Growth principles, but is not meant as a polemic against Church Growth. Rather, it should be viewed positively, as a rigorous theological activity in which the gospel and biblical patterns of ministry are brought to bear on topics to which the Church Growth movement has given a high profile. These are the topics the movement is forcing pastors in all denominations, including my own, to study and consider.

---

[23]This outline is suggested by Wagner, *Church Growth: State of the Art,* pp. 16-18. Wagner describes four basic issues raised in Donald McGavran, *The Bridges of God* (The United Kingdom: World Dominion Press, 1955): (1) The theological issue of God's will for his church to make disciples, (2) the ethical or "pragmatic" issue, (3) the missiological issue that deals with people movements and the homogeneous unit principle, and (4) the procedural issue that deals with discipling and perfecting. The last issue is important, but within the Lutheran context it doesn't have as important a place as in Reformed theology. When the gospel contains the law as in Reformed theology, the question automatically arises as to how much ethical content your gospel should carry with it. In other words, how much sanctification should result prior to the person's full acceptance as a Christian. This concern largely becomes a moot point when acceptance of the gospel is faith in Christ's forgiveness. A confession of faith in Christ's forgiveness makes a person as much a Christian as he or she ever will be. The ethical issue enters afterwards when the person is growing to live his life as the Lord wants him to. This Lutheran emphasis leads to a procedure in missions that does not get stuck on "perfecting" but carries on the work of "discipling" at the same time. In this regard, the Lutheran understanding of the gospel has a built-in antidote for what McGavran saw happening in the churches in India which resulted in his discipling/perfecting issue.

[24]See C. Peter Wagner, *On the Crest of the Wave* (Ventura, Calif.: Regal Books, 1983) for a Church Growth discussion of the charismatic spirit.

119

10.

THE DESIRE TO GROW

The issue as raised by Church Growth

The desire to grow is perhaps the most fundamental of the issues Church Growth has raised. What should be the attitude of the pastor and people about the growth of the church? They answer: The pastor and congregation should want the church to grow.

This may sound like a correct and rather basic answer. But there is quite a bit more to the issue than a basic question and a simple answer. At issue is the question of what sort of mindset a pastor should have about the growth of his church.

Donald McGavran was trained in a liberal seminary and worked with the United Christian Missionary Society.[1] The growth of the churches among which he

---

[1] Yale Divinity School. C. Peter Wagner, ed., *Church Growth: State of the Art* (Wheaton, Ill.: Tyndale, 1986), pp. 22,23.

worked was slow. He came to believe that barriers to the growth of his church were twofold—structural and attitudinal. McGavran worked in the context of a mission station that had become a fortress sealed off from the rest of the society. He states, "A mission with a college, high school, hospital, ten missionaries, budget of $80,000, and seven congregations whose aggregate membership remains less than a thousand year after year is no rare sight."[2]

His complaint was that this setting separated some of the people physically, and most of them economically and culturally, from their neighbors. Attitudes had developed in that setting that only perpetuated the nongrowth. He writes:

> Examining the evidence, I came to believe that a major factor in the slow growth of the church was a massive build-up of defensive thinking and rationalizations. Excuses were piled one on top of another. . . . Christians were walled off from seeing the possibilities and opportunities. They were, unfortunately, comfortable in their courtyard of nongrowth.[3]

McGavran set out to fight these attitudinal and structural barriers to growth. His attitudes toward growth and non-growth are rather difficult to systematize.[4] He writes with excitement and zeal, and his desire for growth, coupled with his experiences with negative atti-

---

[2]Donald A. McGavran, *Understanding Church Growth* (Grand Rapids: Eerdmans, 1970), p. 296.

[3]Donald A. McGavran and Win Arn, *Ten Steps for Church Growth* (San Francisco: Harper and Row, 1977), p. 2.

[4]For a complete discussion of the ecclesiology of Church Growth, see Charles Van Engen, *The Growth of the True Church: An Analysis of the Ecclesiology of Church Growth Theory* (Amsterdam: Rodopi, 1981), pp. 1-47, 324-403.

tudes toward growth, contribute to a penchant for strong statements. He compares the growth of the church to the growth of a child:

> Church development is like that of a child. Adequate nutrition, a maturing social awareness and intelligence are desirable elements in development; but were a child's weight to remain at fifty-six pounds for several years, the mother would rightly feel anxious, no matter how socially mature the child was![5]

His books and the books of his co-workers maintain the conviction that growth is a part of the nature of the church. Win Arn writes, "A basic conviction of the Church Growth movement is that effective evangelism produces measurable results—people discipled and added to the Church."[6] The movement is based on the expectation of growth. McGavran says:

> If the church is preaching the good news of God's power to needy people, if it is concerned about church growth, if it is thinking about church growth, if it is praying about church growth, if it enlists people in the growth of the church, there is no reason why it shouldn't grow. You see, God wants his lost children found.[7]

A person who has done extensive research into this foundational principle of church growth is Charles Van Engen, who states:

---

[5]Donald McGavran, *How Churches Grow* (New York: Friendship Press, 1966), p. 16. (First published in the United Kingdom in 1959.)

[6]Win Arn, ed., *The Pastor's Church Growth Handbook* (Pasadena: Church Growth Press, 1979), p. 98.

[7]Donald A. McGavran and Win Arn, *How to Grow a Church* (Ventura, Calif.: Regal Books, 1973), p. 4.

As far as the Church Growth Movement is concerned, numerical growth is an essential ingredient of its "missionary elan," its ecumenical perspective, its social scientific methodology, and its management principles. It will also be observed how numerical growth is correlated with Church Growth's perspective of the Church's faithfulness to the mission of God in the world.[8]

Arthur Glasser, a close co-worker of McGavran's, substantiates Van Engen's findings:

God wills the growth of His church. . . . Only through the deliberate multiplication of vast numbers of new congregations all over the world will the church be able to evangelize this generation. When she ceases to perform this mission, something fundamental is lost in her very essence as the people of God in the midst of the nations. The church that does not grow is out of the will of God.[9]

This statement is important. It reflects the early thought of the Church Growth Movement well. As Van Engen points out, Church Growth people are making numerical growth one of the "marks" of the Church.[10]

We must bear in mind that this emphasis of the Church Growth Movement is not a trite preoccupation with numbers. Rather, it is a stance that grows out of

---

[8]Charles Van Engen, *The Growth of the True Church* (Amsterdam: Rodopi, 1981), p. 363.

[9]Arthur F. Glasser, "Church Growth Perspectives," *Theological Perspectives on Church Growth,* ed. Harvey Conn (Phillipsburg, N.J.: Presbyterian and Reformed Publishing Co., 1976), pp. 30,31. I credit Van Engen for directing me to this article.

[10]Van Engen, *The Growth of the True Church,* p. 379.

their interpretation of the Word of God, and their understanding of Christ's command to go and make disciples of all nations, which they understand as God's promise that growth will occur.[11] Church Growth's preoccupation with numbers stems from a theological complex that, among other things, states that God has commanded men to disciple the nations. In short, Church Growth states that God has promised numerical success; therefore we are to expect growth in all periods of church history.[12] This is the foundation on which Church Growth rests.

McGavran made his statements in reference to the third world. He made them in view of the many people who have not heard the gospel and because many churches had become entrenched in a mission station mentality that was not suited to reaching out. American Church Growth, however, deals with a country where there are churches in every town. The question of expectancy of numerical results has been modified somewhat. For example, Peter Wagner states his four criteria for successful growth:

> *Axiom One:* The pastor must want the church to grow and be willing to pay the price.

---

[11]Ibid., pp. 374,375.

[12]Church Growth is somewhat ambiguous on this issue. McGavran does not deny that there are some places where the church is not growing, and he submits to that reality. In fact, what appears to some as an overt preoccupation with numbers is really only a statistical study to determine where there are "receptive" and "resistant" segments of the population so that effort can be concentrated on the former and the latter "held lightly." On the other hand, Church Growth is quite short with those who say that growth is not possible. They accuse them of making excuses, and point to other denominations that are growing in the same area. They point out that theology has little to do with growth and sociology has everything to do with it. We will say much more about this in subsequent chapters. I point it out now to substantiate the statement above that when Church Growth theory bears on the individual church, there is an insistence that we are to expect growth.

124

Axiom Two: The people must want the church to grow and be willing to pay the price.

Axiom Three: The goal of the evangelistic outreach program must be to make disciples.

Axiom Four: The church must not be suffering from a terminal illness.[13]

These axioms underscore McGavran's basic thesis of the right to expect church growth. They also exhibit a degree of sensitivity to places where circumstances might inhibit some churches from growing. While this is a concession, notice that it is not a theological concession, but rather a sociological one. McGavran's principle on a theological level remains untouched.

Before one can use Church Growth materials he must come to a conclusion regarding this issue. We must put this question to the Scriptures.

The attitude of the apostles toward numerical growth

I will state my conclusion at the beginning: Church Growth does not err in expecting growth. Rather, it errs in omitting from its discussion certain facets of scriptural teaching. These overlooked facets are necessary for shaping a proper attitude among missionaries and evangelists, as they carry out the work of building the church.

Scripture teaches a paradox in this area that we need to recognize, if we are to achieve the proper mindset for evangelism work. The paradox is this: God teaches that

---

[13]C. Peter Wagner, "The Four Axioms of Church Growth" in Class Notes for Church Growth I, Fuller Theological Seminary (1987), pp. 1,2. For a brief analysis of "terminal illnesses," see Kent R. Hunter, *Foundations for Church Growth* (New Haven, Missouri: Leader Publishing Company, 1983), pp. 112-116.

we are to expect growth, and that we are to expect resistance.

God desires all people to be saved. And, humanly speaking, that desire should be carried out—if God is all powerful, that is. We are to forge ahead and expect that his desire will come true. On the other hand, the Bible teaches that people will resist God. Such resistance does not necessarily result from poor strategy, ineffective communication, or any of the missionary's faults, but on the hearer resisting the sovereign God when God comes to him with the gospel.

Scripture will not allow us to hide behind the rock of a no-growth mentality (Church Growth agrees with this point). Nor will the Lord let us think that part of the equation is in our hands, giving us the power to program growth by doing everything right (Church Growth disagrees with this point). Only the Lord knows when people will come to faith and when they will resist.

This paradox must be recognized and allowed to inform our attitude toward mission work. Lutherans know that if they resolve the paradox in theology, the essence of Lutheranism is lost and what results is Calvinism or Arminianism.[14] Lutherans should also realize that if they resolve the paradox in missiology, there is the same result.

In their writings and in their missionary work, the apostles reflected this paradox.

First, they acted in a spirit of expectancy, and rightly so. Jesus had spoken in positive terms about the growth of the church. He said that on Peter's confession of faith "I will build my church" (Matthew 16:18). Referring to the Gentiles, Jesus spoke about "other sheep that are

---

[14]For a full discussion of the "crux theologorum," see Francis Pieper, *Christian Dogmatics,* vol. 2 (St. Louis: Concordia, 1950), pp. 3-52 and Siegbert Becker, *The Foolishness of God* (Milwaukee: Northwestern Publishing House, 1982), pp. 193-224.

not of this sheep pen. I must bring them also" (John 10:16). His commission to the disciples to "go and make disciples of all nations" certainly carries with it the understanding that the disciples were to expect converts to the faith. Jesus told Paul he was sending him to the Gentiles, to "open their eyes and turn them from darkness to light" (Acts 26:18). Paul promised the Romans he would come to them, "in order that I might have a harvest among you, just as I have had among the other Gentiles" (Romans 1:13). Paul told the Colossians that "all over the world this gospel is bearing fruit and growing" (Colossians 1:6). We might also note several passages in Acts that talk about the numbers of people who came to faith (Acts 2:41; 4:4).

Second, along with a spirit of expectancy, the apostles lived and worked under a total denial of their ability to effect conversion. They knew that people resisted their work and would continue to do so. This understanding was much more profound and complete than the Church Growth understanding of resistance. The apostles understood the total inability of the human heart to accept God's forgiveness. They understood that the only reason a person would be saved was because God had predestined him or her from eternity and had worked faith in his heart through the word. This resulted in focusing their ministry on preaching the word rather than on the desire to grow, even though that desire certainly was present.

The nature of the gospel forced them to acknowledge that only through the Spirit and only by the grace of God was anyone saved. While they expected growth, they also expected rejection. The rejection they expected did not lead them to a down-in-the-mouth attitude about the gospel, or into a sinful posture of pessimism about God's will or power to bestow forgiveness. But it did temper their attitude about growth—particularly about their place in God's plan and what burden or responsibility they should carry toward the growth of the church or lack of growth.

Paul clearly states his understanding of sinful human nature. He states that "nothing good lives in me, that is, in my sinful nature," (Romans 7:18), and that "the sinful mind is hostile to God. It does not submit to God's law, nor can it do so" (Romans 8:7). Earlier in Romans he had described the natural man in these words, "there is no one who understands, no one who seeks God" (3:10).

Among the apostles, there was complete dependence on the Spirit of God in the work of conversion. In 1 Corinthians 2:14, Paul writes, "The man without the Spirit does not accept the things that come from the Spirit of God, for they are foolishness to him, and he cannot understand them." Throughout his letters, Paul thanks God for granting faith to his hearers and for sustaining that faith. The teaching of God's election to faith (predestination) is predominant in the thinking of the apostles. In Romans 9:16, Paul says, "It does not, therefore, depend on man's desire or effort, but on God's mercy." And the first chapter in Ephesians overflows with gratitude to God for bringing the Ephesians to faith, "For he chose us in him before the creation of the world to be holy and blameless in his sight" (1:4).

The early church lived with these various elements that combined to form their attitude toward growth. The first evangelists lived with a paradox. They knew that God wanted all to be saved, and that his intent was to create his church by bringing people to faith in the gospel. They also knew that man could resist God. They did not know how man could resist the power of God working in his heart through the word, but such was the case.

To state it another way, the apostles accepted that it was a mystery why some were saved and not others. This mystery existed not because of the complex (but discoverable) nature of the Spirit's work, but because of the spiritual dynamics at work in heaven and on earth that human reason cannot fathom. Rather than try and answer the question—which would have given them an answer to the question of what to expect concerning growth—the apostles lived in the tension of that paradox.

They could have resolved this tension in one of three ways. They could have resolved it by a static no-growth attitude, or pessimism in the face of resistance. But that would deny the Lord's statements that he *will* build his church. They could have resolved it by a "charge" attitude, in which human powers of persuasion and choice are the touch points for growth. But this would deny the fact of man's total depravity and our total reliance on God's grace. They resolved this tension in a third way. They didn't worry about actual growth or lack of it—although they certainly wanted God's word to produce fruit. They simply did what they were able to do—preach the Word.

The very nature of the gospel led the first Christians into an approach to growth that centered not on a striving for growth per se, but on a striving to preach the word. They knew this would result in growth. But their understanding of the various facets connected with a correct understanding of the gospel did not allow them to develop a misplaced concern for growth or the lack of it. It forced them simply to preach the gospel and let the Lord take care of the results.[15]

---

[15]A basic Church Growth principle is 3-P Evangelism: presence, proclamation, and persuasion. In this area also we see the effect of Evangelical/Reformed theology. It separates the Spirit from the Word of God. The power of the word to convey the forgiveness of sins through the message of the gospel is supplanted by the evangelists ability to make the person see his need for moral renewal. Hence, within the Evangelical mindset, only two attitudes are possible. Either the person presents the word on a "take it or leave it basis" or enters into the process of conversion with his own ability as a persuader. The evangelist's conversion experience has demonstrated to him the benefits

The Lutheran Reformation stressed that the marks of the church were the preaching of God's Word and the scriptural administration of the sacraments. Growth must come through the power of the gospel. Charles Van Engen pointed out that Church Growth actually makes growth a mark of the church. He objected to this and suggested an alternate "new word" (the equivalent of a mark of the church). After quoting from Isaiah 55:11-13, where God promises that his Word would not return to him void, Van Engen writes:

> As a means of pointing to this essential aspect of the Church's nature, it is important to suggest a "new word" which will portray the movement, the feeling, the expectation, the fulfilled incompleteness of this life-force. . . . [The Church] is

---

of faith in Christ because he has witnessed the empirical results in his life. He now needs to "persuade" others that such a change can take place in them, too.

Lutheran and biblical teaching center on the fact that the Word itself contains the power to convert. It also points out that anyone who is convinced he is a sinner and knows God's forgiveness will of necessity present the word in a persuasive way, as did the apostles (e.g., 1 Corinthians 4:11). But he realizes that the message of the cross is foolishness to those who are perishing. While he is persuading, he is at the same time acknowledging that the real work of disciple-making is being done by God through the Word. In other words, even in the area of persuading, he remains within his "circle" of responsibility. And he can do so because he knows the persuasive power of the Word. He relies not on the power of the law to effect a moral transformation, but on the power of the gospel to penetrate the hearts of his hearers with the message of forgiveness. His persuasion does not violate the paradox by itself entering into the equation, other than as a messenger of the gospel.

Charles Van Engen writes, "Possibly if the Reformation theology of the Word were given its full weight as the efficacious means by which God gathers His Church, the presence-proclamation-persuasion discussion would not amount to much. . . . And if it is true that God's Word never returns without producing fruit, then the proclamation is itself persuasion. We might say that the Word itself, in the preaching of the Gospel, was for the Reformers all of that—presence, proclamation, and persuasion combined." (Van Engen, *The Growth of the True Church*, p. 250.)

happy and satisfied because of having its roots deep in good moist soil. Yet it is not quite finished, not at all static, while it yet strives to achieve greater breadth and height and deepness of root. For the want of a better term, we would suggest the "new word" called "Yearning for Numerical Growth" as a means of pointing to the life-principle of which we have been speaking.[16]

While this is a departure from McGavran, it is only a variation on a theme. I have quoted Van Engen so that I can clarify my position by contrast. I believe that the Reformation marks of the church are adequate not only to denote where the true church exists, but also what her emphasis is in reaching out in evangelism work. Neither "numerical growth," nor "yearning for numerical growth" adequately describes the mark of the true church. Rather, "teaching the word and administering the sacraments" (whether in established churches or in evangelism work) is a perfectly adequate description. This is what the church focused on in the apostles' day and what it should be focusing on in her desire today to fulfill the Lord's command to make disciples.

Reformed theology and the desire to grow

Church Growth advocates emphasize only one side of the paradox. They correctly state that God wants his church to grow, but lacking a solid understanding of the accompanying teachings, they use the statement that "God wants growth" to impel them forward into their mission. Consequently, the goal of growth becomes the center, rather than proclaiming the gospel.

What leads Church Growth into this emphasis? I believe it follows from the Evangelical/Reformed under-

---

[16]Van Engen, *The Growth of the True Church,* p. 488.

standing of the gospel. First, they resolve the paradox of why some are saved and not others through an Arminian emphasis on man's ability to decide for Christ by his own power. In this way, they free themselves from the paradox, and give themselves a theological position on which to insist on growth as something people *can* achieve and will want to achieve if they love God. Second, when the gospel shifts off-center to mean a moral regeneration of some sort, the spiritual limits imposed on the gospel by its corollary teaching of "by grace alone," are stripped away. In other words, when the gospel is viewed as the power to "turn one's life over to God and keep his law," the growth of the church taps into a natural desire that even the unbeliever has—the desire to overcome problems which he sees coming from his sins. Once this is done, man does indeed have the power to devise methods to make the church grow. As a result, missionaries are more easily drawn away from their message and concentrate on methods that tap into the latent power in man to come to faith.

I believe this is the dynamic behind McGavran's statements about numerical growth. To say that McGavran or the Church Growth Movement is not sincere about wanting to serve the Lord would be totally unfair. But the nature of their gospel has altered their paradigm for evangelism. This makes it easier for them to center on the bare goal of numerical growth, rather than on the tool itself that God has given us to use so that he can bring about the growth of his church.

Conclusion

It's my conclusion that Church Growth is wrong to focus on bare numerical growth. A scriptural understanding of the gospel and related teachings will lead to the goal of preaching the Word of God and taking our eyes off of growth per se.

This is not a no-growth excuse, even though it may seem to be such to Church Growth people. It is a valid paradigm for evangelism. It neither rules out joy when God brings people into his church nor negates the desire to see the church grow. It is a paradigm by which our mind is centered exclusively on how to preach the gospel. In this paradigm, the means do not justify the end. In our sphere of responsibility, the means are the end. The ultimate end for which we hope and pray—the conversion of souls—is God's responsibility.

11.

VISIONS AND GOALS

The numerical growth of the church and total commitment to numerical growth form the skeleton of Church Growth. "Fleshing out" of this skeleton takes the form of visions, goals, and methods.

In this chapter we'll review Church Growth thinking on this subject. We will also suggest an alternate way of looking at these processes, when they are informed by Lutheran theology. We shall see what place visions, goals, and methods take in the work of the church, as Church Growth understands it. How they use these tools is indigenous to Evangelical/Reformed theology, particularly as it is taught at Fuller's School of World Missions.

Two models for ministry

Like the last chapter, this chapter will be rather abstract. Consequently, before we continue, it will be helpful for us to visualize the points I am raising. I am including two diagrams that will help us see the difference I was talking about in the previous chapter and the difference we will discuss in the present chapter.

The first diagram depicts a Lutheran understanding of ministry. The large circle bounded by a solid line is our sphere of responsibility. Its parameters are established by the gospel of God's forgiveness of the world and our duty to tell others about what God has done for them, so they can receive the benefit of it now and in eternity. The large dot in the center of the circle represents the fact that this understanding of justification is fixed and immovable. It is here that we pin all our work. The arrows

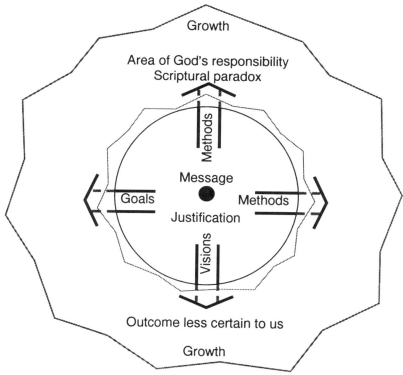

represent goals, visions, and methods. We work with these concepts, but only within the sphere of our understanding of justification. In other words, we work within the sphere of our understanding that the nature of the gospel forces us to focus on *preaching* the gospel.

It is within these parameters that we must devise goals, visions, and methods. Outside the circle we enter into the area of God's responsibility. The lines there are rather crooked. This does not mean that God's plans are broken, or that the goals he wants to achieve are not certain. Rather, it represents the fact that from our perspective God's plans and goals are not firm enough for us to understand and relate to in our programs. Outside our circle lies the paradox we must acknowledge in all our thinking about the final goal of our ministry. There God has the right to shape and direct our plans according to his will. Only if we have constructed our plans within the circle of our responsibility, we will be fluid enough to shape and adapt our plans and to handle success and failure.

What this diagram also illustrates is that Lutheran theology does not preclude visions, methods, and goals. Nor does it undermine our desire to see the lost saved— numerical growth, if you will. It places the entire matter in the proper perspective by anchoring it to the gospel and relating our activities to the nature of the gospel. In short, it forces us not to go beyond our responsibility. At the same time, it forces us to maintain a desire to find the lost.

The second diagram illustrates what is happening in Church Growth and how its thinking is joined with the Evangelical/Reformed understanding of the gospel. As we have seen in Part One, the understanding of the gospel in Reformed circles is more diffused. It pertains to the moral betterment of people and society. This makes the message less clear and more nebulous. The boundary of the meaning of the gospel becomes hazy, and therefore one's understanding of the limits of his responsibility and area of planning becomes less clear.

Moreover, the paradox is lost. In the Church Growth Movement, with its Arminian emphasis, the paradox is lost in the direction of giving people the power to apply themselves to God's grace. Man's natural desire for betterment is tapped into. Missiology becomes less a matter of proclaiming God's word and more an exercise in touching that natural desire in man—or finding the door prepared by God's "prevenient grace." This compromises the gospel as the power of God. The missiologist suddenly finds himself having the "power" to reach people, if only he does the right thing.

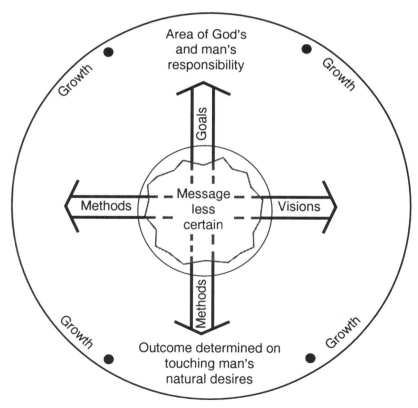

As a result, man moves outside the circle of the gospel of God's forgiveness. When this emphasis is joined with the desire to grow, the pin that fixes one's center is moved from the circle of the gospel outward to the growth that God claims he desires. The growth of the church becomes the fixed object toward which the church is to pull itself, rather than the gospel serving as the fixed object which impels the church forward. This is represented by the solid line that bounds the area of "growth" and by the pins that fix this as the center of the church's work.

When growth becomes the center of the church, methods are conditioned by how much growth they achieve, rather than by the nature of the gospel. This is not to say that methods become totally relative to growth. But the tendency is there.

No church falls totally in one or the other category. Many Evangelicals who identify with the Church Growth Movement still hold to a measure of the objective message of the gospel and attempt to center their message on it. And Lutherans face the strong temptation to move out of the solid circle of the scriptural understanding of the gospel and into the realm of activity that God has roped off for himself. After all, it gives us a sense of control and it suits our desire to diffuse the gospel and make it serve our natural desire for morality.

Visions and goals

Visions and goals in Church Growth

Because of its shift in emphasis, the Church Growth Movement places a high priority on visions and goals, but not within the sphere of responsibility that God has given man as understood by Lutherans. In *Understanding Church Growth,* Donald McGavran stresses the importance of goals: "Nothing focuses effort like setting a goal."[1] He elaborates,

> In Acts the eighteenth chapter we read, "He (Paul) argued in the synagogue every Sabbath and persuaded Jews and Greeks. When Silas and Timothy arrived from Macedonia, Paul was occupied with preaching, testifying to the Jews that the Messiah was Jesus. . . . The Lord said to Paul one night, "Speak and do not be silent."
>
> In view of these passages it is difficult to hold that deliberate plans for persuading men to become followers of Jesus and for incorporating them in churches are in any sense impious. Setting membership goals is in accordance with God's eternal purpose. Goal setting in the service of the Great Commission is pleasing to God.[2]

Speaking of the history of the movement, McGavran states that his colleagues Peter Wagner and Vergil Gerber continued the work of impressing on the world that goals were needed if the work of the church was to be done.

> Walls were about to be built on the theoretical and theological foundations which required open acknowledgment of countable Christians as a legitimate indication of faithfulness in Christian Mission. Peter Wagner and Vergil Gerber played the key role in building those walls—seeing goal setting as a necessary strategy of evangelization and demonstrating how to carry it out.[3]

---

[1]Donald A. McGavran, *Understanding Church Growth* (Grand Rapids: Eerdmans, 1980), p. 412.

[2]Ibid., p. 417.

[3]Ibid., p. 421.

Central to the matter of goals was the idea of "faith projections" which are "estimates as to what growth God is going to grant this congregation, or denomination. . . ."[4]

But "faith projections" or "faith goals" are really more than estimates. In fact, they contain a power in themselves. What was more or less implicit in McGavran's enthusiasm for goals—that they are a power for the growth of the church—is explicit in the writings of modern Church Growth leaders. Peter Wagner in writing about Robert Schuller states:

> Possibility thinking boils down basically to a synonym of what the Bible calls "faith." Schuller's definition of possibility thinking is "the maximum utilization of the God-given powers of imagination exercised in dreaming up possible ways by which a desired objective can be attained." He is convinced that "the greatest power in the world is the power of positive thinking."[5]

Wagner continues, "God wants us to be bold. He wants us to take risks for Him."[6]

Charles Chaney and Ron Lewis define visions and goals. They write:

> What is a dream or a vision? It is a mental picture of a future reality. In the context of Christian discipleship and church growth, our frame of reference, we are interested only in Spirit-inspired dreams and God-given visions. Therefore, if the leadership of your church has no dream for your church, begin to ask God immediately to

---

[4]Ibid., p. 427.

[5]C. Peter Wagner, *Your Church Can Grow* (Ventura, Calif.: Regal Books, 1976), p. 58.

[6]Ibid., p. 57.

140

share his purpose for your church with them. From this perspective a vision becomes a kind of promise of what is to be. It is an image of the divine intention.[7]

What is a goal? A goal is a response to a perceived need. It, too, is an image or picture of what the future might be or how it might be shaped. It is a future event that can be accomplished and towards which you can make measurable progress. . . . it may reflect or express a God-given dream, but it must be achievable and is, therefore, measurable.[8]

Such definitions express precisely what Church Growth means when it uses those terms. Charles Chaney and Ron Lewis write, "It will be impossible for your church to get out of its holding pattern without a dream."[9] Win Arn points out the power Church Growth sees as inherent in goals.

When a person sets a measurable goal for him/herself, the likelihood of reaching that goal increases. This well-documented behavioral principle has increased productivity in workplaces, changed deviant behavior in clinical counseling patients, helped over-eaters reduce their calorie intake. It's also a behavioral principle that can help you help your members in their Christian life and growth.[10]

---

[7]Charles L. Chaney and Ron S. Lewis, *Design for Church Growth* (Nashville: Broadman Press, 1977), p. 78.

[8]Ibid., p. 80.

[9]Ibid., p. 78.

[10]Win Arn, "How to Increase Your Worship and Giving by 10% or More," *The Win Arn Church Growth Report* (Number 25).

141

As Church Growth becomes allied with the charismatic movement, the concept of visions as direct revelations from God becomes more pronounced. One of the leaders of Church Growth's charismatic connection is Paul Cho who describes the importance of visions in his theology:

> There is no obstacle that can discourage a man who has been given a vision by the Holy Spirit. . . . Once God has granted you a vision, then you must learn to spend time dreaming over that vision. This is the essence of my Christian philosophy. It covers all of the principles of church growth work. I call it "visions and dreams."[11]

Visions and goals in the Scriptures

The term "vision" is a Biblical term. It refers to direct revelations from God to a person. The question we want to ask of Scripture is this: What visions were given to the early church leaders and what was the substance of those visions?

Scripture does give accounts of people to whom God gave visions. The Lord appeared to Stephen when he was being stoned (Acts 7:55), to Philip as God led him to the Ethiopian Eunuch (Acts 8:26ff), to Saul at his conversion (Acts 9:3ff), and to Ananias to lead him to Saul (Acts 9:12ff). He appeared to Peter to show him that the Gentiles were not to be considered unclean (Acts 10:9ff), to the church in Antioch to tell them to commission Paul and Barnabas for mission work (Acts 13:2), to Paul when God told him to go and preach to the Macedonians (Acts 16:9,10), and to Paul once more, telling him that the Lord had many people in Corinth whom he was going to bring to faith (Acts 18:9,10).

---

[11]Paul Y. Cho, *More Than Numbers* (Waco: Word Books, 1984), p. 21.

142

Some of these visions related to the spread of the word and the growth of the church. And all these visions, except that given to Paul in Corinth, contained specific directions about where or to whom to preach the word.

There is a complete absence, however, of any instructions or examples of people or churches receiving visions giving them a mental picture of what their church would be like in the future—which was to impel them forward in their work. In 1 and 2 Timothy, books written to a pastor, there is no hint that Paul expects Timothy to pray for or expect such a vision.

Nor did Paul ever intimate that he sought visions of what to expect from his missionary work. The one time he received a vision about numbers, he was simply told by God that he—namely, God—had many people in Corinth (Acts 18:10). The purpose of this vision was not to lead Paul to set numerical goals. Rather, the Lord wanted Paul to take courage in the midst of persecution. God was comforting Paul with the assurance that his work was not terminated in that city. The only thing Paul was told to expect was "prison and hardships" (Acts 20:22,23).

What about goals? The idea of numerical or "faith" goals is not found in Scripture. I realize that an argument from silence is not the best, but you would think that if visions and goals were such an important part of God's plan for his church and if he wanted us to rely on the dynamic of numerical goals to achieve growth, he would have suggested it somewhere in the New Testament.

On this point one cannot appeal to the technological advances we enjoy in our century and to the notion that Paul did not have our technology. The issue of visions and goals is quite basic. The businessmen of Paul's day certainly had goals, and Paul could have learned from them if he had wished. But nowhere—especially in 1 and 2 Timothy—where we would expect to see such advice, do we find it. On the other hand, in the one place in the New Testament that talks about businessmen who seek to achieve certain quantifiable goals, all the Lord does is censure them for their presumption (James 4:13-17).

An analysis of visions and goals

My concerns regarding visions and goals are related to those regarding the desire for numerical growth, as that desire has surfaced in the Church Growth Movement. At the heart of this issue lies the paradox that must remain intact if we are to maintain our understanding of the gospel as objective justification. We know that God wants all men to be saved and that he alone saves them. We know that people can resist his will. But we do not know why one person is saved and another lost. Nor can we penetrate the mystery by placing the blame on God or giving credit to man.

As soon as we decide to use visions, we force ourselves into one of two positions. (1) We must proclaim, as do many in the Church Growth Movement, that they have received their vision directly from God (e.g., Paul Cho). (2) Or we must understand that our vision is, by God's permission, based on our subjective imagination (e.g., Robert Schuller).

In the first case, the paradox is maintained. For we are given the answer to the puzzle directly by God himself. If someone can show that he has received his vision from God, he can in good conscience pursue its fulfillment. On the other hand, if he maintains that it is indeed a product of his imagination, then he has already admitted that he has found the answer to the paradox in that the amount of growth is directly proportionate to the amount and kind of his effort—and that he will achieve the results his vision anticipates. In brief, to adopt a subjective vision implies that one knows the equation of why some are saved and others are not.

The same applies to goals. As Chaney and Lewis point out, goals are visions quantifiably perceived.[12] When goals are made in the area that God has left for himself, those goals lead us away from our paradox, and invariably into the Evangelical mindset. The issue does not revolve around whether a person has zeal to win the lost. The issue revolves around whether that zeal is confined to the area of our responsibility or whether we move outside of it. The result is that in the former case, the integrity of the gospel is maintained, while in the latter it is compromised.

Is there a place for visions and goals and the planning that must accompany them? I would say, yes. But referring to the diagram I presented at the beginning of this chapter, Lutheran and scriptural theology leads us to have visions within the "circle" of our responsibility. Visions become objective, even though they may be personal. They are objective because they enable us to "see" ourselves *preaching the word* in one way or another. To envision a method that reaches people with the message of forgiveness, to envision a church building in a city where God is gathering people into his church, to envision a program to help people study or teach God's Word —are all visions that rest on the work God has given us to do.

Visions can be personal also. God directs various people into different situations and then leads them to attempt something for him. This applies to both the religious and the secular world, as Paul shows when he told the Athenians, "From one man . . . [God] made every nation of men . . . and he determined the times set for them and the exact places where they should live. . . .

---

[12]Chaney and Lewis, *Design for Church Growth,* p. 80.

For in him we live and move and have our being" (Acts 17:26-28).

God gives people "visions" of what they are to do. These form a sort of blueprint from which to work. People establish goals and they plan to accomplish what the Lord has given them to do. When vision is thought of in this way, it is within the scope of what a human being can do. The subjective element in these visions and goals will always be tempered with the humble prayer, "Lord, if you will."

In the work of the church, visions, goals, and planning must be related to the preaching of the word. I believe that the absence of talk about visions and goals in 1 and 2 Timothy underscores this fact. No one would accuse Paul of not being growth-oriented. But in the only letters where anyone is ever commanded to "do the work of an evangelist" (2 Timothy 4:5), all the emphasis on what that evangelist is to do lies in the area of preaching the word. Paul writes to Timothy, the evangelist:

> Until I come, devote yourself to the public reading of Scripture, to preaching and to teaching. . . . Be diligent in these matters; give yourself wholly to them, so that everyone may see your progress. Watch your life and doctrine closely. Persevere in them, because if you do, you will save both yourself and your hearers. (1 Timothy 4:13,15,16)

Applications for the ministry

My concern is to remain within my circle of responsibility. This concern will be reflected in the way I use visions and goals, planning and persuasion. This understanding precludes establishing percentage or absolute "faith goals" as a tool to bring about the growth of the church.

The teaching of justification by faith will remain the place where my work is "pinned" and, while I want to grow, I will concentrate on the message itself. This means using visions, etc., as structures within which I can become more effective in *preaching the word*. It will limit the scope of my planning to *preaching the word*.

12.

FELT NEEDS—
THE MAIN TOOL OF CHURCH GROWTH

When Donald McGavran objected to the way mission work was being done in India where he worked with the Disciples of Christ, he was objecting to the classic mission compound system. In this system, according to McGavran, Christians were taken out of their native setting, brought under the influence of the mission compound, and given all the benefits of Christian schools and medical facilities. In this context, their social status was "lifted"[1] and because of this they had difficulty maintaining intimate contacts with their own people. This resulted in missions that lost touch with the unbelieving community, and it made it impossible for them to begin and nurture "people movements."[2]

The concept of people movements and its theoretical underpinning in the homogeneous unit theory are basic

---

[1]Donald A. McGavran, *Understanding Church Growth* (Grand Rapids: Eerdmans, 1980), pp. 295ff. McGavran's discussion of "halting due to redemption and lift" forms the introduction to his people movement and homogeneous unit theory.

[2]Ibid., pp. 333ff.

148

to McGavran's thought. Without the homogeneous unit theory, Church Growth would not be Church Growth.

In this chapter, I will attempt to describe this theory and show that it finds expression in American Church Growth in two areas—"Web Evangelism" among friends and relatives and "Felt Need Evangelism" among those who have no formal contact with church members. We will spend most of our time on the latter concept.

Homogeneous unit theology

McGavran observed that many Christians who lived in mission stations experienced social isolation from their countrymen. This isolation hindered evangelism, both because it kept present Christians away from their neighbors, and because it forced would-be Christians to take a dramatic step in the direction of these isolated Christians. Such a step would almost surely mean estrangement from family and friends.

McGavran established a two-sided theoretical approach to the problem. As an antidote to how the mission stations separated the Christians from their fellow countrymen, McGavran suggested the "people movement," or "web movement," approach to evangelism. As an antidote to the dislocation new Christians felt when they left their friends and relatives to become Christians, McGavran suggested the homogeneous unit principle. Although these principles are different, they are related. Wagner calls the homogeneous unit principle a corollary of the people movement theory.[3]

Both principles begin with one of McGavran's most frequently quoted statements, "Men like to become Christians without crossing racial, linguistic, or class barriers."[4]

---

[3]C. Peter Wagner, ed., *Church Growth: State of the Art* (Wheaton, Ill.: Tyndale, 1986), p. 17.

[4]McGavran, *Understanding Church Growth,* p. 223.

When this statement serves as a basis for one's missiology, what results is a very heavy emphasis on the sociological dimensions of the growth of the church. We will examine Church Growth's sociological emphasis in chapter 13. This emphasis on sociology, however, leads to the two principles mentioned in the preceding paragraph and to other sub-principles.

McGavran's basic argument in his earlier book, *The Bridges of God*,[5] is that the growth of the church takes place along natural bridges. These bridges are the contacts Christians have with non-Christians. The use of these bridges results in many people coming into the church. Such an activity is called a "people movement." McGavran defines it:

> A people movement results from the joint decision of a number of individuals—whether five or five hundred—all from the same people, which enables them to become Christians without social dislocation, while remaining in full contact with their non-Christian relatives, thus enabling other groups of that people, across the years, after suitable instruction, to come to similar decisions and form Christian churches made up exclusively of members of that people.[6]

This definition of people movements contains much of the homogeneous unit principle. That principle states that the gospel spreads more rapidly among people who share something in common. People movements occur most easily within homogeneous units.

What constitutes a homogeneous unit is difficult to pin down. Wagner states that if the distinguishing char-

---

[5]Donald McGavran, *The Bridges of God* (The United Kingdom: World Dominion Press, 1955).

[6]Ibid., p. 335.

acteristic of a homogeneous unit is "cut too thin," the division loses its helpfulness as a sociologically distinct unit from the standpoint of the growth of the church.[7] He defines a homogeneous unit as a group of people who "feel at home" with each other; "they know they are among 'our kind of people.'"[8]

These two principles that McGavran "discovered" have had tremendous implications for American Church Growth. McGavran was mainly interested in mass movements of people into the Christian church. But Church Growth has translated this emphasis into methods that it encourages average American churches to use.

The principle of "web movements" has been adapted and disseminated by Win Arn, head of the Institute for American Church Growth. His main tool is the Chuck Bradley film series that portrays a typical Christian couple who learn to use their natural bridges of friends and family to spread the gospel. The basic point Arn teaches is that people feel more comfortable in a church when they know people who attend there. Arn calls the method *"oikos"* (household) evangelism.[9] The "web movement" principle is the homogeneous unit principle with family ties being the thing that the group holds in common.

The main evangelistic strategy: felt needs

Felt needs theory

From the homogeneous unit theory comes an emphasis that has dominated the American church scene. It cannot

---

[7]C. Peter Wagner, *Our Kind of People* (Atlanta: John Knox Press, 1979), p. 75.

[8]Ibid.

[9]See Win Arn and Charles Arn, *The Master's Plan for Making Disciples* (Pasadena: Church Growth Press, 1982), pp. 46-49 for a diagram of how *oikos* evangelism works.

be called a product of the Church Growth school, but it is a method that has been adopted by them as a perfect expression of their emphasis on using sociological structures to foster growth. It has almost come to be the hallmark of the American Church Growth Movement—at least on a popular level. When the average pastor taps into Church Growth, the first thing he is likely to come away with is a program to discover the felt needs of the community.[10] Indeed, Peter Wagner writes:

> There is no such thing as a patent medicine that will cure all of the ills of man and beast, nor is there any universal method of evangelism that will help a church to grow.
>
> As to the basic principle for discovering the proper method, though, I would have a hard time improving on Robert Schuller's maxim: *The secret of success is to find a need and fill it.* The methods used in growing churches, diverse as they might be, have all done this or they wouldn't be working. They have offered something which meets the needs of the kind of people they are ministering to.(emphasis his)[11]

That this is an outgrowth of McGavran's homogeneous unit theory is clear from what Peter Wagner

---

[10]A qualification is in order at this point. The statements and analysis about felt needs that follow are more accurate of the Church Growth thinking of the late 1970s. Today, the felt need emphasis has been coupled with the charismatic spirit and accompanying signs and wonders. "Power Evangelism" has replaced felt need evangelism in the sense that it is a higher expression of the principle. The charismatic spirit is viewed as a more powerful method of meeting people's needs. In more conservative denominations, the classic felt need theory is still the key issue. This is the issue that is important for consideration in my denomination and therefore will be our focus.

[11]C. Peter Wagner, *Your Church Can Grow* (Ventura, Calif.: Regal Books, 1976), p. 160.

writes, "Every different homogeneous unit has a different set of needs. You will have a difficult time detecting people's needs if you do not know their homogeneous unit. Worse yet, if you don't, you might find yourself offering people solutions to problems they don't even have."[12]

The felt needs emphasis is defined as, ". . . the conscious wants and desires of a person; considered to be an opportunity for Christian response which stimulates within the person a receptivity to the gospel."[13]

Chaney and Lewis expand on the importance of the felt needs emphasis. Any church wanting to grow must take into account the needs of people it is trying to reach. They assert that "no plan for church growth can ignore 'people needs.'"[14] They go on to say, "People who are lost from God and his plan for their lives must become the focal point of strategy planning. These plans must be large enough to include a variety of needs as well as meeting the need for a spiritual relationship with God."[15]

Churches are encouraged to discover what their community considers to be its main problems and then devise programs that address those problems within the context of the gospel message.

Felt needs methodology and the Evangelical / Reformed gospel

On the following pages, we will discuss the felt needs theory within the context of the nature of the gospel. I believe that the felt needs theory as understood by

---

[12]Ibid.

[13]Wagner, *Church Growth: State of the Art,* p. 290.

[14]Charles L. Chaney and Ron S. Lewis, *Design for Church Growth* (Nashville: Broadman, 1976), p. 35.

[15]Ibid., p. 36.

Church Growth is a direct outgrowth of Reformed theology and that it is antithetical to Lutheran theology.

The conclusion we came to at the end of Part One was that Reformed theology focuses on moral improvement and on the difference in life that Christianity brings. Reformed theology sees the gospel as the power to become something rather than as the declaration of God's forgiveness. This emphasis is distinct from the Lutheran emphasis on the forgiveness of sins as the central thrust of Christianity.

Felt needs theory is cast within the context of gospel as a "power to become." As such, it is totally consistent with current Evangelical/Reformed theology. In other words, it is a completely valid methodological expression of the theology of its source.[16] To illustrate this, we will examine the thoughts of various proponents of felt needs theory.

In his book, *The Contagious Congregation,* George Hunter III discusses the changing mindset of people in the modern secular world.[17] He encourages churches to keep the following changes in mind when they devise evangelism strategies.

The first change is from knowledge to ignorance. People simply don't know that much about Christianity.

The second change is from a concern over death to a concern for life. Hunter states, "To a greater or lesser degree people are now asking questions like, How do you cope in this life? How do you make sense out of this

---

[16]We will limit our discussion to the type of felt need methodology that flows from mainline evangelical churches. More liberal churches may use that term, but they use it as an equivalent of the social gospel. Evangelicals use it in relation to regeneration and in the context of the gospel as power for renewal.

[17]George Hunter III, *The Contagious Congregation* (Nashville: Abingdon, 1979), pp. 91-103. Hunter draws from Donald Soper, The Advocacy of the Gospel (Nashville: Abingdon, 1961).

life? How do you get along with people? How do you find meaning and purpose?"[18]

The third and most important shift is from guilt to doubt. He writes:

> If you have the luxury of speaking to people who now want forgiveness, you will find this to be a relatively easy communication task because their response will come fairly readily. But, if you are speaking to people whose major obstacle to faith is doubt, you will find evangelizing them a more difficult and protracted process.[19]

Fourth, the shift has led from "a sense of need for Christianity to a sense of curiosity about Christianity and Christians."[20]

Finally, people who used to feel a sense of belonging in the world now feel a sense of alienation.

Hunter's question is, What implications does this have on the way the gospel is presented? He writes, "The foregoing analysis raises many questions. How do you get the gospel across? How do you help people discover the rescuing and fulfilling possibility that God extends to them through Christ's church?"[21]

In the ensuing discussion, Hunter states what methods he believes the modern mindset calls for. Central to his methodology is discovering what people need:

> We must first demonstrate the relevance of our gospel by beginning where people are in their conscious needs and motives. Having demonstrated the relevance of what we are about to

---

[18]Ibid., p. 93.

[19]Ibid., p. 94.

[20]Ibid., p. 94.

[21]Ibid., p. 97.

share, thereby winning their attention, we then plug in the facet of the gospel that is relevant good news for the need or motive that has been engaged.[22]

Notice how Hunter views the gospel. It is not the message of forgiveness, but consistent with Evangelical/Reformed theology, it is a multifaceted concept that is wide enough to supply help to any given need or problem. Hunter then states what the facets of the gospel are that apply to modern secular society.

For those who are more life-oriented and less death-oriented and are looking for meaning in life, Hunter says, "[We] commend this message: In Christ and his mission through the church you can find your meaning! Christ is the clue. Following him leads to meaning."[23] For those who are alienated the message is, "you are known and loved."[24] To those who are alienated from their world, "we must proclaim that there are Christian causes to which you can give your life, causes that are of the essence of the kingdom of God, and if you'll give your life to those causes you can make a difference."[25]

Notice that in the process of speaking to the needs of people, the message of forgiveness is not a factor. Rather, whatever emphasis in forgiveness may have been present in Hunter's theology is supplanted by those "facets of the gospel" that speak to people's current need. This is the Evangelical/Reformed gospel, and Hunter's methods are consistent with it.

Chaney and Lewis express a similar concern for meeting people at the point of their felt needs. They state

---

[22]Ibid., p. 100.

[23]Ibid., p. 101.

[24]Ibid.

[25]Ibid., pp. 102,103.

that an evangelist must focus on the audience and not just on the product. This is because "people do see and hear what they want to see and hear. Everyone has what has been called a 'God-given filter.'"[26] They state, "Only when the message is addressed to the felt need in an individual is that filter open so the message can get through."[27]

But what is the message according to Chaney and Lewis? It is not the Lutheran message of God's declaration of forgiveness, but the Reformed message of God's power to help in the crises of life. They write:

> The church that discovers where people are hurting and meets that need in the name of and with the message of Jesus Christ deserves to succeed. The big question is not, How can we get these people to accept the message? That is the wrong question! The big question is, Where are these people conscious of pain and how is Jesus Christ good news to that situation? What can we do to heal the open wounds and throbbing aches of the people in our community?[28]

Again, the message of Christ is a message of help to the pains of life, rather than a message of pardon from the pains of the law's condemnation.

On a more popular level, felt needs theory is expressed especially in the context of family life problems and needs. This is the most popular arena for development of felt needs ministries. Flavil Yeakily says:

> New Testament Christianity has the only viable answer to the family problems this nation and

---

[26]Chaney and Lewis, *Design for Church Growth,* pp. 74,75.

[27]Ibid., p. 75.

[28]Ibid.

the people in it are experiencing. The church has something very valuable to offer the community. . . . If Christianity can offer people in the community help in improving the quality of their family life, they can minister in a way that no one else can.[29]

This latter emphasis has given rise to a large number of family life seminars that has become the method of attracting people to the church.

Felt needs and its effect on the gospel as God's forgiveness

It is clear that the gospel as understood in the Evangelical/Reformed church is compatible with evangelism methods that use the felt needs of people as their beginning point. If the gospel is the good news that by God's power a person can become something, it is only natural that the evangelist ought to discover what the person needs to become.

But what about the Lutheran understanding of the gospel? Is it compatible with the felt needs emphasis? I believe that the answer to that question becomes clear when we look at several more statements by Church Growth experts. These experts themselves do not consider the felt needs emphasis to be compatible with a gospel that is essentially a declaration of forgiveness. While they are reacting to the propositional truths of more historic Evangelical/Reformed theology, their statements apply to Lutheran theology as well.

Win and Charles Arn write:

---

[29]Flavil Yeakley, "A Profile of the New Convert: Change in Life Situation," *The Pastor's Church Growth Handbook,* vol. 2, ed. Win Arn and Charles Arn (Pasadena: Church Growth Press, 1982), p. 36.

There is strong research evidence to indicate that new Christians who accept Christ and continue as responsible church members first perceive the gospel message in terms of its relevance to their own lives. Evangelism training which relies on "canned" presentations, memorized testimonies, and universal spiritual dictums has difficulty responding to the unique needs of the non-Christian in terms of his/her day-to-day experience and the resources available in Christ.[30]

Notice how the Arns draw an antithesis between felt needs evangelism and other forms of evangelism that view evangelism as the declaration of "universal spiritual dictums." In doing this, they are striking at the heart of the Lutheran understanding of evangelism, which builds on one "dictum"—that all people are sinners—and proclaims that Christ has died for the sins of the world. To the Arns, the gospel has become the idea that "resources" are available to help with life's problems.

Robert Orr describes sources of prospects for the church and lists those who have moved into a new neighborhood as being good candidates. In recommending the felt needs approach as the way to contact them, he admits that

this, by the way, is a subtle but significant shift from the traditional visitation goal of many churches. Previously the goal has been to present the gospel in every home and endeavor to get a decision for Christ. A new approach, however, would see a community visitation program as a way of finding prospects, and then developing a

---

[30]Win Arn and Charles Arn, "The State of Evangelism in America," *The Pastor's Church Growth Handbook*, vol. 2, p. 13.

strategy to reach each person or family on the basis of their particular needs.[31]

While Lutheran evangelism does not seek to lead people to decisions as that term is understood by the Evangelicals, the gospel message to them is something to be
proclaimed. In being consistent with the Evangelical/Re-
formed definition of the gospel, Orr relativizes it around
the needs of the people and is not unaware of the fact
that he is advocating a new kind of evangelism.

Russ Reed, an advertising executive highly respected
by Church Growth, states that when a church advertises, it must reach people at the point of their felt needs.
He establishes an antithesis between doctrine and the
point at which the non-believer is to be reached. He
states that we must know what we believe, but "when
we're communicating with people who are not a part of
the inside group, we need to change our language so
they understand what we are talking about."[32] If Reid
means that we must talk in terms clear to our listeners,
he is correct. But he does not really mean that. Earlier
in his article he stated, "What is the promise of the gospel? Have you ever asked that question? I struggle with
it a lot. My theory is that the promise of the gospel cannot be understood in propositional terms. It can only be
understood in relational terms."[33]

By relational, Reid means a relationship with Christ
in which a person receives the power to change his life.
That is the Evangelical/Reformed gospel. In that context, there is no problem in separating doctrine from
outreach. The point of need to which the "gospel" is ap-

---

[31]Robert Orr, "How to Develop a Prospect File . . . and Use It Effectively,"
The Pastor's Church Growth Handbook, vol. 2, ed. Win Arn, p. 49.

[32]Russ Reed, "A Strategy for Media and Your Church," *The Pastor's
Church Growth Handbook,* vol. 1, ed. Win Arn, p. 124.

[33]Ibid., p. 123.

plied can be understood in terms other than those used by Scripture.

But when the gospel is a propositional message of what God has done for the world in Christ, such a separation becomes impossible. I believe Reid would admit that if the gospel is propositional, the felt needs emphasis is not compatible with it.

The felt needs emphasis reaches its logical conclusion in Robert Schuller's ministry. Wagner writes approvingly about Schuller:

> He rarely quotes the Bible because he did a research project some years ago and discovered that unchurched people in Orange County don't believe the Bible. So he directs his sermons to their felt needs such as their family, their job, their financial situation, their self-esteem or their emotions, explaining how Jesus can meet those needs.[34]

Wagner concludes, "If you can serve a diet of positive sermons focused on the real, felt needs of the people you will be preaching for growth."[35]

The Lutheran must realize that it is not just a matter of how much or how little he chooses to use the felt needs approach. The point is that the felt needs approach, as taught by Church Growth, stems from the Evangelical/Reformed understanding of the gospel. As such, it is antithetical to the Lutheran and scriptural understanding of the gospel as a propositional truth that people appreciate only when they come to know the guilt of their sin.

---

[34]C. Peter Wagner, *Leading Your Church to Growth* (Ventura, Calif.: Regal Books, 1984), p. 177.

[35]Ibid., p. 218.

13.

FELT NEEDS STRATEGY

Felt needs and Scripture

In the last chapter we made the point that the felt needs emphasis as taught by Church Growth leads to a Reformed understanding of the gospel and is antithetical to the gospel as the message of God's forgiveness. In this chapter, we will see that Scripture does not support this emphasis. Rather, through instruction and example, it teaches that evangelism work must be done through the law and the gospel of God's forgiveness in Christ.

The woman at the well

We begin our examination of Scripture with those passages most often used as examples of the felt needs theory. The passage most often referred to is John 4— the story of Jesus talking to the Samaritan woman at the well.

It is commonly claimed that Jesus appealed to her felt needs, when he asked the woman for a drink of water and then shaped his discussion around the idea of an artesian well. It's said that this is similar to the felt needs theory of ministry as we have examined it in the previous chapter. Is this so?

Clearly, Jesus used something the woman happened to be doing at the time of their encounter. He began the discussion by asking her for a drink of water (John 4:7). After the woman questioned his sincerity and motives, he responded, "If you knew the gift of God and who it is that asks you for a drink, you would have asked him and he would have given you living water" (John 4:10).

The conversation continued. The woman was interested. She requested this living water.

Jesus immediately shifted the topic under consideration. He addressed her sin. He told her to get her husband and bring him. The woman felt guilty. She tried to dodge her guilt by denying that she has a husband. Jesus agreed with her, but in the process exposed the fact that she had had five husbands (John 4:16-18).

Does this account support the felt needs theory? The way Jesus begins his discussion with the woman bears a certain resemblance to it. But the resemblance is superficial. Jesus did not come looking for the woman's felt need. Nor did he establish any program to assist the woman in doing her daily task of coming to draw water. What he did was use an event in her life—something that was on her mind—to introduce his message. This point of contact was no more than that—a point of contact.

If there is a lesson to be learned from this account, it's that we should be open to looking for points of contact on which to build a discussion of the law and gospel.

This is exactly what Jesus did. He pointed out her sin. He told her he was the Messiah, the promised Savior. To read into this account the felt needs theory of Church Growth is exegetical dishonesty. The fact that the discussion had gone only a few minutes before Jesus exposed the woman's sin tells us that Jesus' strategy was completely different than Robert Schuller's, for example, who avoids saying anything negative in his sermons. Jesus preached the law to the woman, from the beginning of their encounter.

Jesus took a chance. The woman could have walked away. But his chance paid off, for he could point to himself as the Messiah and know that when the woman believed him, she was recognizing him for who he was— her Savior from the guilt of sin.

Becoming all things to all men

Paul's statement in 1 Corinthians 9:19-23 is the second most popular section of Scripture to which the felt needs theory appeals. In this section, Paul utters the well-known words, "I have become all things to all men so that by all possible means I might save some" (1 Corinthians 9:22).

Those who espouse the felt needs approach claim that Paul's statement of becoming all things to all men meant that he developed his ministry programs around the needs of his hearers. But is this what Paul was referring to?

The first two categories he goes on to list are the Jews and Gentiles. He "became like them" to win them. Perhaps we could envision some sort of Messianic synagogue, or a church intended specifically for the Gentiles and their needs.

But the third group Paul speaks of gives us some difficulty when we apply it to the felt needs theory. Paul states that he became weak so as to win the weak. How does one develop a program for the felt needs of the weak? I can't recall anywhere in Church Growth litera-

164

ture where weakness was one of the felt needs discovered through door to door canvassing. Nor do I recall any suggestions for developing a program for the weak. It might be said that any program to reach people in their emotional or social weakness constitutes "becoming weak." But there is no hint that Paul had social or emotional weaknesses in mind when he spoke those words. Rather, coupled with the concepts of "Jew" and "Gentile," weak must mean weak in knowledge—the same kind of weakness he spoke of at length in Romans 14:1—15:13.

Even in the case of Jews and Gentiles, we find no evidence that Paul created separate churches for them, or that he developed different programs for their spiritual growth based on their felt needs. In every case, Paul preached to them the same message of Christ as their Savior from sin.

What Paul means is that he strove to understand the thoughts of the Jews, Gentiles, and the weak, so that he could approach them with the gospel of forgiveness in such a way that they understood what he was saying. In a spirit of humility, he literally *became* a Jew or a Gentile and did what was hardest of all—he became weak to those whose understanding was far weaker than his own.

To the Jew he talked as Jesus talked to Nicodemus, using his background to rebuke and to teach him. To the Gentiles he put himself in the place of people who had served idols their whole life, and he rebuked and taught them in that context. (See the account of Paul in Athens, Acts 17:22ff.) He tried to do the same thing Jesus did when he dealt with the woman at the well. He did not push the weak along too quickly or assume they knew more than they did.

He looked for a point at which he could begin his message. And we can be sure that he quickly got into his message. Always, the message was the same. As in the story of the woman at the well, Paul's words fit the felt needs method only superficially.

The jailer at Philippi

Occasionally, the account of the jailer at Philippi is referred to in support of the felt needs theory (Acts 16:16-34). The story, however, supports the view that Paul's idea of ministry was a ministry of the message of forgiveness.

The jailer was about to kill himself. Paul and Silas told him not to. He then asked, "Sirs, what must I do to be saved?" (Acts 16:30) What did this man mean by salvation? There is only one possibility. He had already heard that the prisoners were all there. He was not worried any longer about salvation from the Roman sword. He must have heard Paul and Silas singing and praying the day before and heard enough to know that they had a God who had given them hope and salvation. He wanted to know about their God. His felt need was the need to know about Christ and his salvation.

Most likely he still retained the idea that he had to *do* something to be saved. The apostles simply told him the good news about Jesus. The jailer didn't need to *do* anything, but simply *believe* in Jesus and be saved.

The miracles of Jesus

Sometimes the miracles of Jesus are used to show that he appealed to the felt needs of the crowd before he told them anything about his work. Such an appeal to Christ's healings and miracles has become more popular in Church Growth circles since they adopted the charismatic spirit.

Here, too, the similarity between what Jesus did and what Church Growth advocates do is only superficial. There's no question that Jesus and the disciples performed miracles. Those miracles most often dealt with the physical needs of the people—for healing and for food. But why did Jesus perform miracles? He did it to show that the kingdom of God had come. Satan would be defeated through Jesus' suffering and death on the cross.

At no time did Jesus ever look for the felt needs of people and then shape his ministry accordingly. He helped people because he loved them. Throughout his ministry, he was sensitive to the possible misuse of his acts of mercy. He continually warned people who had witnessed or benefited from his miracles not to tell what he had done, lest others get the impression he was merely a bread King. (See John 6:1ff.) He wanted them to repent of their sins and believe in him as the suffering servant of God, who had been sent to die for them and to rise so they might rise. At the expense of his popularity, he rejected those who praised him because of his miracles. What a contrast to those who want the church to grow by using people's felt needs and who develop programs to draw them on that basis!

Recall the points we made in Part One, when we looked at the sermons the apostles preached throughout the Gentile world and the methods they used to establish churches there. They preached the cross of Christ. There is no evidence of their searching out the felt needs of their potential converts. They came to each town with the "message of the cross." They did not make their message understandable by changing it into the power of God that would change people's lives at the point of their felt needs. Rather, it was a message of God's pardon and peace, a message that was "foolishness to those who are perishing, but to us who are being saved, it is the power of God" (1 Corinthians 1:18).

Such a message was powerful. It opened people's hearts to believe in Christ's forgiveness and find themselves at peace with God.

Lutheran theology and the felt needs approach

A decision each pastor and evangelist must make is how to approach the unbeliever. How he approaches the issues raised in this chapter and in the last one will determine his strategy and will, to a large degree, determine his relationship with current Evangelical/Reformed evangelism.

Although I will continue my discussion of the Church Growth Movement for another two chapters, it is here that I will address the crux issue that places one either inside or outside the Church Growth camp. This is the basic evangelism question with which conservative Lutherans must continue to wrestle. There can be no room for ambiguity on this issue. Either the felt needs approach is the best way to do evangelism work or it is a tool that is inherently dangerous to the gospel message understood as the message of the forgiveness of sins.

Lutheran evangelism is undergoing difficult times, largely because of the teachings of the Church Growth Movement. It has caused a lot of hesitation on our part. It has raised doubts about our abilities as evangelists; it has caused confusion about the nature of our message.

I say this not to criticize the Church Growth Movement per se, for it is totally consistent with the theology from which it springs. The inconsistency lies with us Lutherans. What Lutherans are attempting to do is combine traditional methods based on the nature of our gospel with the methods of Church Growth. We are attempting to use the entry point that the Reformed use when they lead someone to accept their gospel, while at the same time to retain our gospel. We hope that somewhere between the time people enter our churches through the Church Growth entry point, and the time they become members, they will come to understand that the gospel is not an infused power for more moral living, but that it is the message of forgiveness that gives peace to a heart troubled by the guilt of sin.

To use David Luecke's phrase, we are attempting to use Evangelical style and maintain Lutheran substance, a practice which he heartily endorses.[1] Another Lutheran educator, though, is not quite as confident as Luecke seems to be that a marriage between the two can be effected. Wayne Stumme, an ELCA educator at the Lutheran Theological Seminary, Columbus, Ohio, squarely faces the fact. In an address to Missouri Synod Lutherans he states:

> The Church Growth movement, generally speaking, was developed by conservative Evangelicals. And it is my tentative observation that the movement itself tends to produce that type of church: a "conservative Evangelical" church in terms of piety, in terms of theology, in terms of social attitudes, also in terms of congregational life. What does this mean for a confessional church like the Lutheran Church? Not every method is equally appropriate; not every method can be domesticated or "Lutheranized." What kind of transformation would occur if, say, the Lutheran Church-Missouri Synod went completely into the Church Growth Movement and adopted its assumptions? That's an interesting question for you to deal with. You may have a more hopeful and positive answer than I am prepared to offer. . . .[2]

A century ago the English playwrights Gilbert and Sullivan wrote an operetta in which they poked fun at

---

[1] David Luecke, *Evangelical Style and Lutheran Substance* (St. Louis: Concordia, 1988).

[2] Wayne Stumme, "A Lutheran Critique of the Church Growth Movement." A taped lecture from the 1988 Lutheran Exegetical Theology Symposium at Concordia Seminary, Fort Wayne, Indiana.

the "esthetic poets" who wrote poetry three times a day and whose languid expressions and morbid affectations were capturing the affections of the ladies. The ladies, who had been engaged to a group of soldiers the year before, had broken off their engagements and were madly in love with a poet, Reginald Bunthorne.

After a while, the soldiers decide the only way they can win back their ladies is to become poets themselves. So they dress up like poets and sincerely try to copy all the right postures and mannerisms. They find, however, that their background of soldiering has not prepared them for the mannerisms of an esthetic.

The Major exclaims, "It's quite clear that our only chance of making a lasting impression on these young ladies is to become as aesthetic as they are."

To which the Colonel replies, "No doubt. The only question is how far we've succeeded in doing so. I don't know why, but I've an idea that this is not quite right."

What often happens is that Lutherans who try to Lutheranize Church Growth methods, particularly the felt needs approach, begin to feel that same way. They don't know why, but they have an idea that something isn't quite right. Not having the theological background from which Evangelical methods have sprung, Lutherans can only produce a rather stilted imitation.

A conservative Lutheran congregation that attempts to use felt needs methodology finds itself struggling with its theology on various points. Felt needs methodology is based on the presupposition that God wants people to "receive" him and his regenerating power. Finding the problems in life that people are aware of and promising help sets the stage for the reception of the Reformed gospel. And only the reception of the Reformed gospel will satisfy the person who has been brought into the church through the felt needs approach.

Sometimes it happens (and I do not blame the prospects for this) that when a Lutheran church opens the felt needs door and those who enter do not find a spirit compatible with their desire to "change their lives" in the sense they anticipate, they leave.

Effects of the felt needs approach
It transposes law and gospel

The felt needs approach switches around the basic theological presupposition that forms the very essence of Lutheranism. It transposes law and gospel. Rather than teaching law and gospel in that order, love itself (both human and divine) is used first to try and make the object copy that love himself and so find a blessing for his life. Outside the context of first preaching God's justice, the "tug" of love is the moving force that leads the prospect to desire the *ability to love,* and so to find meaning and fulfillment in his life.

Without the proper preparation that the condemning nature of God's law affords, the gospel cannot maintain its nature as a declaration of forgiveness. Instead, it becomes a power for renewal. Once this love is received into the heart in the form of a distinct experience, renewal then becomes possible. The decision to "repent"— that is, to put off sin or to give up the natural resistance to God—is a condition that fulfills the requirements, if "Christ is to enter the recipient's heart" and begin his work of "regeneration." Once this power establishes itself as part of the recipient's faith, it becomes a day by day struggle to continue the work of repentance if that power is to remain.

This problem arises in the misuse of "friendship" evangelism. Friendship evangelism is as old as Christianity. It is often through the "web" of friendship that the message of the gospel flows. But in its modern use in Church Growth, it is not the message of God's love that

171

spreads. What spreads is the message that "you can become loving like me" if you become a Christian.

It changes the nature of sanctification

The felt needs approach changes the nature of sanctification. In Scripture, sanctification is the response the believer gives to the Lord who has forgiven him all his sins. In the felt needs approach, however, sanctification becomes the means to fulfill the prospect's needs for acceptance, fulfillment, and a better life through victory over sin. Sanctification, then, becomes man-centered rather than God-centered.

The nature of Christian love also changes in the context of this type of evangelism, at least for Lutherans. Rather than loving a person and helping with whatever needs he or she may have, in the felt needs approach love is used to effect conversion. Also, the evangelist turns the person's needs into a lever by which to bring him into the church. What's more, it becomes difficult (and in some cases dishonest) to "shift gears" and use the opportunity afforded by felt needs to present a gospel that is not implied in this approach.

Toward a Lutheran position

How should we view the matter of felt needs? I think we have to consider a number of things. We must consider the nature of the gospel and our duty to proclaim it, the natural depravity of the human heart, and God's providence in dealing with all people but especially with the elect. We also should draw a clear line between the Church Growth felt needs approach and a solid biblical point of contact approach.

Preach the gospel and depend on God's providence

We begin with God's providence. Does God use the felt needs approach? In his providence we must answer, yes.

Sometimes God brings an unbeliever under the influence of the law and gospel by using felt needs. In the process, God brings him to see that he has a greater need—peace from the guilt of his sin.

In his wisdom and power, God can use the entry point of the Reformed gospel and lead a person to hear the real law and gospel and lead that person to faith in Christ's forgiveness. Granting that, we must underline the fact that God is the one operating in this way. Nor is this an artificial distinction. All evangelists make this distinction and draw the line at some point between God's providence at work and the methods they believe God has given them to work with. Throughout the ages, God has brought people into the church in some pretty amazing ways—ways that no evangelist would dare try to copy.

Some of the statements we must make on this issue are similar to those we made in the chapter on visions and goals. We saw that the Church Growth Movement steps outside of the bounds of responsibility God has given us and moves into God's area. We are aware that God uses various means to bring people under the influence of the gospel and that he uses various means to point out to people the fact of their sin. But this awareness should be tempered by the fact that God has given us the responsibility to preach his law and his message of reconciliation.

God can use the ulterior motives of people to lead them into church, but we are not given the license to copy his ways and means. God may use the ills of a person's life to lead him to see his sin, but our message must not copy his to the extent that we imply that Christianity is the means to his overcoming his ills. Our responsibility lies in the work of preaching the word— the word of forgiveness that God will use. When we attempt to copy the methods God in his wisdom uses, we, in our foolishness, will always give people the wrong impression. In the process, we invariably give the gospel a different meaning.

I believe we ought to worry about the work of preaching and teaching, fashion our evangelism work after the overall pattern given us in Acts and other places of the New Testament, and leave the rest up to God's providence.

Acknowledge mankind's depravity and rely on God's grace

How wicked the human heart is! It knows what to do but refuses to do it. In the face of the harm it causes to the body it continues to abuse drugs and alcohol and food and does not stop until it has destroyed a person.

How intent on possessions the heart is! It can lie in a nursing home at the age of eighty, with only months left to live, and still be more concerned about the few pennies a neighbor stole than about hearing the message of forgiveness through which the greatest of all riches can be found.

How hard and stubborn is the human heart! It can witness every form of God's wrath against people who suppress the truth about him, and yet still want to revel in sin and cheer on others who are joining in (Romans 1:18ff).

When the Bible says "no one seeks God" (Romans 3:11) and "the sinful mind is hostile to God" (Romans 8:7), we must take such words at face value. Certainly, no one is closer to coming to faith than anyone else, unless the Holy Spirit awakens faith in a person's heart.

Many Lutherans will admit that no one is closer to coming to faith than anyone else, but, they contend, because of circumstances in the lives of some, those people may be closer to wanting to hear the gospel. At face value this isn't right either. To want to hear the gospel im-

174

plies faith in the gospel already. We might be able to say that some people are closer to wanting to hear something, whatever it might be.

Yet even here we must be careful. As we wrestle with this concept, we need to ask several questions first. Does experience in fact show that more people come into the church as a result of hearing the gospel during a crisis in their lives? Does a crisis situation better establish a feeling of guilt over sin? Is such a paradigm for discovering "prospects" useful for the evangelist? Or might it lock him into a mindset that is looking for crisis situations, rather than being open to the secret workings of the Spirit in hearts where no apparent crisis is taking place? Most importantly, does such an emphasis inadvertently lead to turning Christianity into a crisis solving religion?

However we answer these questions, we must be careful about giving the impression that one person is "closer to the gospel" than another. If anyone is closer to hearing the gospel than another, it is only because God has elected him to come to faith and at the right time will bring that faith into being.

While God's providence may be viewed as a process, conversion itself is not. The human heart remains totally unyielding in the face of its sins and sufferings, until the Holy Spirit creates faith in the law and gospel in a person's heart. Would it not be better to develop a mindset that seeks to capitalize on every opportunity that comes our way, crises or non-crises, realizing that God will work when and where he wills? In other words, when conversion is viewed in a Lutheran sense, is there any practical merit to human indicators of who may be a better prospect? In my opinion, it is of no practical value and only tends to get in the way of a healthy mindset toward evangelism. We realize we are not to cast pearls before the swine. At the same time, we will not withhold the opportunity to hear the law and gospel simply because someone doesn't fit into the "likely prospect" category.

Recognizing this will enable the evangelist to use the term "pre-evangelism" properly. In some circles this term is more consistent with Reformed theology, in which the desire for morality and its concomitant conversion experience is seen as a process originating from within the good of human nature. Lutheran theology views this activity as coming from the *opinio legis* rather than from God's Holy Spirit in action. "Pre-evangelism" is more in tune with the idea of prevenient grace as being an initial work God does in the human heart, drawing the person to God even before he has heard the gospel.

One Reformed writer describes the concept of prevenient grace in relation to evangelism like this: "John Wesley helps his spiritual descendants understand this important truth with his doctrine of prevenient grace. Oversimplified, the point is that before we do our work of witness, God has already preceded us, gently wooing those persons by his Spirit."[3]

This stands in contrast to the Lutheran understanding of prevenient grace as that initial grace God gives as people are hearing the word. Martin Chemnitz, a Lutheran church father, expresses it this way:

> But when prevenient grace, that is, the first beginnings of faith and conversion are given to a man, immediately the battle between the flesh and the Spirit begins. . . . The things which have been said about prevenient, preparatory, and operating grace have this meaning, that the initial stages in conversion are not ours, but God—

---

[3]Harold K. Bales, *A Comprehensive Plan for Evangelism* (Nashville: Discipleship Resources, 1978), p. 12.

176

through the Word and divine inspiration—goes before us, moves and impels our will.[4]

If the term pre-evangelism is used, then let it be stripped of its active meaning as far as conversion is concerned. If conversion takes place by God's grace and God's grace comes only through the word, then anything that leads toward a conversion must be evangelism in the strict sense, where the message of the gospel is communicated. Or, if we mean the term to refer to our activities of love that God can use in his providential work of leading a person to a time and place where he will listen to the gospel, then let us understand this, too, as only preparation for evangelism proper.

A congregation might want to emphasize to its members that "everything we do is evangelism"—that is, everything has a bearing on the ministry of reaching out to the lost. If so, it may want to use the term "pre-evangelism" to separate everything the church does by way of preparation for evangelism from actually speaking the word of God. But even here a warning is in order to avoid the misunderstanding described above.

We must also answer the question of what effect the Christian life has on unbelievers. It's well to avoid using phrases such as, "The life of the Christian is the only book some people will ever read." If that is so, then those people will certainly be condemned, no matter how well that book was written, or how carefully it was read. Rev. Paul Kelm, an evangelist, told the story of a Christian who tried to act his best around his unbelieving neighbor. After giving a consistent witness to his life of faith for many months, his neighbor finally came up to him and said, "You know, I have been

---

[4]Martin Chemnitz, *Loci Theologici*, trans. J. A. O. Preus (Saint Louis: Concordia, 1989), p. 249.

watching you for months, and I want to become like you." The Christian was overjoyed, until his neighbor continued, "Yes, I want to become a vegetarian just like you."

Conversion can never come about unless the law and gospel are present. Our lives are witnesses to the truth of what we believe. When people see us, they are not turned away from the gospel by our sinful lives. When God finally brings them to faith, they give glory to God that such a witness was given to them (Matthew 5:16; 1 Peter 2:11,12). When a believing woman shows the power of God working in her life through her faith, her husband is won over "without words" by her behavior (1 Peter 3:1,2). In this passage, it is unrealistic to think of such a woman not communicating what she believes to her husband, at least at some point in their relationship. Peter encourages her to let her life preach to her husband, that here is a woman who shows the kind of love and moral living that can only come from her Christian faith. This kind of life makes the gospel attractive (Titus 2:10).

I believe it is easy to understand this relation between our lives and the gospel. To try and describe it dogmatically only takes away some of the beauty of this part of our witness. Yet, we must understand it in the light of what the rest of Scripture says about the depravity of human nature and about conversion and the means of grace. We must not wrongly interpret what the Bible says and so get ourselves into the "infused grace" syndrome, as if our lives were acts of grace that fueled the unbeliever's natural desire to become more moral.

Let us preach the gospel. And let our lives bear witness to the righteousness we have by faith. Then everything will fall into place in our evangelism work.

*Give the gospel of forgiveness
and leave the rest in God's hands*

Martin Luther was right when he pointed out that the only way a Christian can preach about blessings is when those blessings are presented as lying behind the cross. He said:

> Divine and true promises immediately point out the cross, but after the cross they promise a blessing. Reason is offended by both: the invisible and far distant things it regards as worthless; but for the cross it has an aversion, and flees from it as from an incessant evil that never comes to an end. And this is why, though God gives abundant promises, only those [believe] whose hearts the Spirit moves, so that, like Abraham, they disregard all dangers and cares and simply cling to the voice of God when He calls them.[5]

Anyone who believes this will begin and end a discussion of his faith with the simple matter of sin and grace. The blessings attached to Christianity mean nothing until the Spirit moves the heart of the listener, and it is only through the law and the gospel that the Spirit works.

The church must always be cautious about how it portrays the blessedness of being a Christian. The "health and wealth" preachers obviously promise people what God does not promise them. Some charismatic healers give people the impression that God promises healing from every evil and that only our lack of faith stands between us and God's blessings. These people clearly warp the nature of the Christian life and what we are to expect.

---

[5]Martin Luther, *Luther's Works,* ed. Jaroslav Pelikan, vol. 2 (Saint Louis: Concordia, 1960), p. 268.

Jesus was much more realistic. He told his disciples about the persecution that would be theirs (John 15:20). He told people to count the cost before they became members of the kingdom (Luke 14:25ff). St. Paul speaks of himself as being filled with anxiety about the spiritual state of his churches (2 Corinthians 2:12,13) and of "wasting away" because of the trials and struggles he was going through (2 Corinthians 4:16).

We can give the impression that Christianity means something other than it is. This can be done in two ways. First, it is done when evangelists hold out promises that the Bible does not say God will keep, such as freedom from some of the problems and anxieties that people face in the modern world. Does God want to free me from them? Yes, but in the same sense as he wants to free me from illness and death and all the other effects of sin. But he has not promised that he will take them away this side of heaven. He may use the stress, anxiety, and other problems people face as tools for his work of chastening. In fact, every Christian can say that he would have fewer earthly problems if he gave up his faith and went along with the world's flow. Secondly, the Christian evangelist himself may understand the deeper meaning of freedom from these problems. But when he assumes that same understanding on the part of the unbeliever in the name of "reaching him where he is," there can be nothing but a misrepresentation of Christianity in people's minds.

We step out of our area of responsibility when we make promises to people on the Lord's behalf that he has not revealed he will keep. Promises associated with the "infused grace" type of Christianity inevitably are only partially fulfilled. The church has been called as God's agent to give the one promise he will always keep—his promise of forgiveness.

This promise alone is certain, as are the peace and joy that flow from it. We stand on solid ground when we proclaim it. Our duty is to lead people to know the pardoning love of God, to nurture them in that love, and to urge them to live sanctified lives. The result of teaching justification as God's declaration of forgiveness is perfect peace for the hearer. Only this promise can be received and guaranteed by faith. According to his gracious will, God will bless that person in this life or, in his wisdom, he may withhold some blessings. Only if people understand that forgiveness and the kingdom of God is the heart and core of their hope will God's dealings with them fall into place and not offend them (Matthew 11:6).

When people come to a pastor for help with emotional or family problems, he must always ask himself what his role is and how he is going to carry it out. If he immediately attaches himself to the needs of the counselee, he may find himself "using" the gospel to help solve the problem. "Let Christ into your life," he might say, "and you will find help." Or, "Christ can give you the help you need if only you will believe in him." We know that God will help us. But those phrases do not get to the heart of the law as God's will that carries with it eternal punishment if not obeyed. Consequently, the real gospel of God's forgiveness cannot truly be proclaimed. I realize how difficult this is as I am faced with these situations all the time. But a pastor must continue to wrestle with the matter, asking himself how he can use a situation to get to the law and gospel, rather than "using" the law and gospel to help the situation. The church body or pastor that ceases to do this will gradually shift his emphasis and tend more toward some type of social gospel.

As Luther says in the quotation above, we must view the blessings of Christianity as lying behind the cross. To me, that implies that any talk about blessings can only be understood by a person who has experienced what Christ's cross means for him. We might put it this way: Both the message of forgiveness and the spiritual blessings accompanying it seem foolish to the unbeliever, and both can be appreciated only by the power of the Holy Spirit.

Draw a line between "felt needs" and "point of contact"

It is important to make a clear distinction between the "felt needs approach" and what we might term "point of contact approach."[6] The former contains elements that are inimical to the gospel. The latter is a desire to find an opportunity to talk about law and gospel by using various situations in people's lives. As we have seen, the "felt needs" approach grows out of the Evangelical/Reformed gospel. The desire for wanting to find a "point of contact" grows out of a heart that wants an opportunity to share the gospel with another sinner. The first is something we ought to avoid. The latter is something the Christian both on the individual and congregational level ought to work hard on.

How does one determine when a program is based on the felt needs approach and when it is merely seeking a point of contact? The matter hinges on one's understanding of faith. Faith that is solidly rooted in an understanding of law and gospel, the purpose of the

---

[6]Using the term "point of contact" does not really solve the basic issues we are wrestling with. The idea of "point of contact" may be nothing more than another term for "felt needs." It is not a change in terms that will solve the problem, but developing a solid attitude about the total depravity of mankind and the nature of conversion, and especially the nature of the gospel. The term "point of contact" as it is used here refers more to a temporal ideal than a topical idea. In other words, it refers to a Christian's looking for any setting in which to share the gospel—a setting which God could give him at any time. This is in opposition to a topical approach that views some situations in life as being more conducive to preaching the gospel to him, even though (and this may or may not be the case) in the normal course of events one's experience may be that crisis situations (either in the life of the evangelist or of the prospect) may afford more opportunities.

church, and the nature of conversion will have no trouble remaining within the proper bounds.

On the one end of the continuum is the classic Church Growth use of the felt needs approach. In this approach the ministry of the congregation (not just its point of initial contact) is tailored to satisfying those needs. To a greater or lesser extent, the congregation becomes oriented toward the social gospel. On the other end of the continuum is the traditional evangelism approach used in Lutheran churches. This includes advertising the message of the gospel, distributing information on the gospel, and praying that the Lord will use the gospel to draw people into the congregation. It includes help and encouragement to individuals in the congregation to use the opportunities they have in their home, workplace, school, and people's homes to bring the gospel to people.

There is a certain gray area, however. This includes congregational programs that may be used properly or abused. A few examples will help clarify the points I am trying to make.

Example: A foreign mission that is intent on preaching sin and grace sets up a medical dispensary because it learns of the tremendous need for medical assistance in the country where it is working. It realizes this dispensary is going to provide points of contact with the people and is looking forward to capitalizing on them. *Comment:* There is nothing wrong with this at all. The dispensary is being set up as a work of love for the people in the community. It will be there for people whether or not they come to church. As long as the message of the mission congregation focuses on sin and grace, there will be no misunderstanding about what the purpose of the dispensary is.

Example: A person has a hobby or an area of interest and decides to form a group of like-minded people. He or she knows that there will be opportunities to witness to

183

the people who are there. It is not long before the group realizes that their host is a Christian and will speak about his faith. *Comment:* There is certainly nothing wrong with this. There is no hidden agenda and there is no danger of confusing this auxiliary activity with the work of the church, especially if done by an individual.

Example: A church begins a Christian day school for the children of its congregation, knowing that many from the neighborhood will be interested in joining. They see this as a potential evangelism tool. *Comment:* If the congregation were to play up the need for a moral education and so appeal to the felt needs of the people in the community, it could be distorting the message of the church. In the context of wanting a Christian day school for members of the congregation, and making the teachings of the congregation known to prospective non-member students and parents, there's nothing wrong with this being a good point of contact.

Example: A congregation realizes that many of its members would like to have a study on what the Bible says about marriage or parenting. The congregation establishes a group and encourages members to invite non-members, realizing that such a group can be a point of contact to the non-member. *Comment:* The congregation needs to be up front that this class is primarily for members who know the law and gospel and who are now seeking instruction from the Bible as to how God wants them to live as his people. The pastor will want to impress on all that the discussion presupposes an understanding of sin and grace; he may use the initial minutes of the class to review the message of law and gospel.

Example: A congregation begins a number of support groups and recreation groups for the community. It starts its own single parents group, parenting group, aerobics class, and softball league. Its purpose is to establish points of contact between members and non-members taking part in these groups. *Comment:* This is different from the previous examples. It is here that I see a danger of a congregation using the felt needs approach even though it may not intend to do so. There are a number of issues involved.

For one thing, when a congregation sets up a support or study group and advertises it as a service to the community, it puts itself in a difficult position. It must make a decision: Are we going to address this group of non-Christians in the same way a secular counselor would address them, or are we going to speak as Christians? In the first case, the congregation has departed from its God given purpose. In the second case, it is assuming that non-members can understand something (the nature of Christian sanctification) they are not ready to understand. This problem is compounded if the non-member comes to worship. Are the sermons and liturgy that center on sin and grace going to appeal to him? Are the pastor and congregation going to begin shifting their emphasis in order to maintain the emphasis under which the non-member first became interested in the congregation? In short, using a support group that involves moral issues as a point of contact will make it difficult for a congregation to maintain its focus on law and gospel. Moreover, Lutheran congregations that use Evangelical/Reformed material to assist in such support groups compound the problem and, in my opinion, make it almost impossible for the situation to be viewed in a doctrinally correct way.

As for the social organizations used in the above example as points of contact, strictly speaking, there are no moral issues involved here. So some of the concerns we just raised do not apply. If the congregation simply acknowledges that its own "in house" social functions can be avenues for the Lord to establish a point of contact with non-members, then there is nothing wrong with this approach. But if the programs are deliberately set up for the purpose of attracting non-members, the church must ask itself whether or not it may be laying a less than solid foundation for the prospective new member to join the congregation. It may be telling him that this activity is at the heart of our congregation's work. In this case, though, much has to do with context and emphasis; there may be situations where this type of program is possible. But the congregation will want to do some soul searching: is it watering down its message, and watering down other more traditional programs of encouraging people to do the difficult day by day witnessing to the gospel, using the opportunities God has given them in their lives?

Ideally, all of the above examples should become less and less important as members grow in a knowledge of their faith and sanctification and "shine like stars in the universe as [they] hold out the word of life" (Philippians 2:15). As a formal program, though, the point of contact approach, as long as it does not degenerate into the felt needs approach, provides congregations with ample opportunities for outreach without compromising the nature of the gospel.

Conclusion

What should we do? I believe we should follow the pattern established in Scripture. Like Jesus and St. Paul, we ought to become all things to all people, in the sense that we understand them and can work with them in the best possible manner. In this way, we will attempt to lead them to know their sins and Christ's forgiveness.

As a parish pastor, I know that some people come to church because their conscience bothers them. Others come for many other reasons. Some desire to serve God because they realize how their rejection of him has wrecked their life. They come with their own agenda, just as we Christians often cling to our personal agendas and desires, rather than to God's.

For this reason, we dare never stand at our church door with a sign that reads, "Only for those who have their reasons for entering well thought out." Nor should we hold a sign that says, "Only for those who feel the guilt of their sin—not for those who come because they are lonely, sick, confused, or feeling the results of their sins." Yet, I don't believe we should be afraid to address people directly with law and gospel, always trying to understand them and always using whatever points of contact the Lord supplies.

We who are ministers and evangelism leaders need to think through our understanding of the gospel and see whether our methods are consistent with it. In love for our fellow men, we will help all who come to us and give them whatever counseling, encouragement, and assistance we can. But our goal as leaders must be to gently shepherd all our prospects into a fuller understanding of God's kingdom. Through the law and gospel, we will seek to lead them away from focusing on how God and his church ought to meet their agenda. Instead, we will work toward understanding that God's wonderful agenda—an agenda that is hidden and often contradictory to what one might consider the "victorious" Christian life—*will* be met for them in time and in eternity. We must take care that the way we establish a point of contact does not hinder our ultimate work.

I have chosen to focus on this key element in American Church Growth thought and bring the Lutheran understanding of the gospel to bear on it. In the next chapter we will broaden our discussion and see that Church Growth in general is based on the premise that social dynamics are the key to the growth of the church.

14.

CHURCH GROWTH AS A SCIENCE

The Church Growth Movement calls itself a science and considers its principles to be scientific in nature. In this chapter, we will consider whether this claim carries with it a scriptural understanding of church and evangelism work and whether it fits in with Lutheran theology.

The movement's view of itself

Next to his statement that men like to become Christians without crossing sociological barriers, Donald McGavran's second most famous comment is, "The great obstacles to conversion are social, not theological."[1] With this statement, McGavran made a radical shift in the way the church viewed itself in relation to the work of

---

[1] Donald A. McGavran, *Understanding Church Growth* (Grand Rapids: Eerdmans, 1980), p. 215.

the Holy Spirit. McGavran's statement set the tone for the way the Church Growth Movement has always viewed itself—as a science.

George Hunter describes the significance of Mc-Gavran's statement: "As he applied the categories and tools of the social sciences to evangelization questions, he quietly ushered Christian evangelism into a new era, similar to the new era in pastoral counseling that came when its leaders began taking the behavioral sciences seriously."[2]

Peter Wagner explains that "the scientific aspect of church growth is vitally interested in understanding and describing all the factors which enter into cases of failure and success in evangelistic efforts."[3] He describes science as "nothing more than an attempt to explain certain phenomena in a reasonable and systematic way."[4] He applies this to Church Growth: "It tries to explain in a reasonable and systematic way, why some churches grow and others decline, why some Christians are able to bring their friends to Christ and into church membership and others are not."[5]

Church Growth views all science as coming from God. In this respect, it carries with it a "cause and effect" world view, in which things happen in an orderly way. Just as "scientific theories help us understand God's creation better," so the science of church growth enables us to understand the growth of the church better.[6] Just as science, though, does not explain everything (at least not at the present time) and is still wait-

---

[2]George Hunter, Forward to *How Churches Grow,* by Donald McGavran (New York: Friendship Press, 1966), p. vii.

[3]C. Peter Wagner, *Your Church Can Grow: Seven Vital Signs of a Healthy Church* (Ventura, Calif.: Regal Books, 1976), p. 43.

[4]Ibid.

[5]Ibid.

[6]Ibid., p. 44.

ing for more information to emerge by which theories can be adapted and made more realistic, so the science of church growth is a matter of observation and discovery.

Church Growth views the growth of the church as a very difficult thing to predict, not so much because of the unknown element in the working of the Spirit, but because of the complexity of his working. McGavran acknowledges that "good judgment and a humble dependence on God who alone gives growth is assumed" in his discussion of homogeneous units.[7] But the reason for his humility is not because the working of the Spirit is inscrutable. Rather, it's because the Spirit's working is quite complex. He writes that "growth is a most complex process" and "God uses many factors *as yet* not understood by us."(emphasis mine)[8] With that mindset Church Growth proceeds in a systematic (and scientific) way to discover more and more elements of the complex way the Spirit works.

Church Growth takes a two track approach to discovering the scientific principles of the growth of the church. First, it observes growing churches and attempts to discover a general pattern of successful methods. Second, it taps into the social sciences to discover what insights they might have in adjusting the structure of the organization so as to promote good group dynamics, effective leadership, and optimum communication. Wagner describes the shift that has occurred in Church Growth thinking. Church Growth is moving from a content orientation to a receptor orientation. Wagner has abandoned the theological debate and has opted for a more pragmatic approach that "looks to social science [as opposed to philosophy] as a cognate dis-

---

[7]McGavran, *Understanding Church Growth,* p. 243.
[8]Ibid.

cipline [to theology] and emerges with a phenomenological methodology which may appear altogether too subjective to many traditional theologians."[9]

We would not agree that philosophy should be a cognate discipline of theology. Theology can stand on its own. What Wagner points out, though, is that using sociology alongside theology is replacing one source of assistance for theology with another. Wagner substitutes sociology for philosophy and chooses to deemphasize what *ought* to be done and concentrates on what *is* working now. (Such is the danger, though, when philosophy has already held a respected place in the doctrinal position of a church body.)

Specific areas of study

Through observation and with help from the social sciences, Church Growth studies various areas. It is beyond the scope of our book to discuss them at any length. Our focus is outreach in the American Church Growth Movement, but it would be well to mention a few of the other areas in order to get a feel for the scope of the movement.

The writings of Church Growth's leading thinker and most prolific writer will serve as a good outline. Peter Wagner's books are both scholarly and practical. Perhaps most basic are his books on church health and church illnesses. In *Your Church Can Grow,*[10] Wagner discusses the seven vital signs of a healthy church. In *Your Church Can Be Healthy,*[11] he prescribes cures to churches suffering from various illness.

---

[9]C. Peter Wagner, "The Church Growth Movement after Thirty Years," *Church Growth: State of the Art,* ed. C. Peter Wagner (Wheaton, Ill.: Tyndale, 1986), p. 33.

[10]Wagner, *Your Church Can Grow.*

[11]C. Peter Wagner, *Your Church Can Be Healthy* (Nashville: Abingdon, 1979).

In *Our Kind of People,*[12] Wagner describes how the homogeneous unit principle applies to America. He debates the melting-pot idea and argues that the sociology of America's ethnic groups supports McGavran's observation that churches grow best when they work within ethnic (or homogeneous) units. In *Church Growth and the Whole Gospel,*[13] Wagner discusses the evidence that points to how churches that keep evangelism as a top priority and maintain a healthy mix of social concern are those that are growing. In *Leading Your Church to Growth,*[14] he discusses the leadership styles that appear to be conducive to the growth of the church. He analyzes the leadership style of various leaders and discusses why they are successful.

The Church Growth Movement abounds in technical terms which might seem strange to the uninitiated but which do, in fact, make sociological distinctions that are valuable within the Church Growth framework. Church Growth defines various types of cross cultural mission work, various types of evangelism work, different types of numerical church growth, and so on. The reader is directed to any of several available glossaries that list these terms and their meanings.[15]

The scientific study of receptivity

George Hunter states, "The Church Growth movement's greatest contribution to this generation's world

---

[12]C. Peter Wagner, *Our Kind of People* (Atlanta: John Knox Press, 1979).

[13]C. Peter Wagner, *Church Growth and the Whole Gospel: A Biblical Mandate* (San Francisco: Harper and Row, 1981).

[14]C. Peter Wagner, *Leading Your Church to Growth* (Ventura, Calif.: Regal Books, 1984).

[15]See Wagner, *Church Growth: State of the Art,* pp. 281-302 for perhaps the most up-to-date glossary. Glossaries are also available in Kent Hunter, *Foundations for Church Growth,* pp. 186-197 and in Delos Miles, *Church Growth: A Mighty River,* pp. 50-59.

evangelization will be its stress upon receptivity."[16] The key area in which Church Growth uses sociology is in the area of outreach. The question is: Is there such a thing as receptivity to the gospel, and can receptivity be forecast, enhanced, or capitalized on?

The other issues we have studied so far are all linked to this issue. The desire to grow as a dynamic for growth can only be understood if we accept the premise that we can discover and find greater success with receptive people. The issue of goals and visions only makes sense if we can "get a handle on" who is receptive and who is not. The matter of felt needs only makes sense if one accepts the presence of pressing felt need to indicate a higher receptivity to the gospel. The Church Growth Movement would acknowledge such an interplay between these issues and would use it as a foundation for strategy.

Donald McGavran takes receptivity to be a given and links receptivity with the scientific approach to the growth of the church.

> How does one know whether a population is responsive? Eventually measurements may be worked out which will tell in advance how ready for new things a given population is. The science of anthropology has learned much about societal conditions in which men are restless for change. The experience of the Church indicates that immigrants in a new country, migrants to a city, societies suffering from deprivation or shock, and the oppressed, hear and obey the gospel more readily than contented beneficiaries of the social order.[17]

---

[16]George Hunter III, *The Contagious Congregation* (Nashville: Abingdon, 1975), p. 104.

[17]McGavran, *Understanding Church Growth,* p. 183.

We agree with McGavran that "unevenness of growth has marked the Church from the beginning."[18] However, is that unevenness caused by a factor we can analyze, explain, and even use in our planning? McGavran answers yes.

> Ministers and missionaries often ask, Are the factors which create receptivity measurable, so that with proper techniques of appraisal we can know that such and such a population is ready for the gospel or is on the way to becoming ready? One keen churchman asked, Could measurements be fed into a computer so that the Church would know exactly the degree of receptivity and whether it was increasing or decreasing? The answers to these questions are "in the distant affirmative." Some day this will become possible. Indeed, today a trained observer can judge with a fair degree of accuracy that a given homogeneous unit is in a state where its members will welcome change.[19]

In all fairness, we should note that McGavran sometimes states that for now, the way receptivity is to be measured is simply by noting where the greatest number of people are coming to faith. He often makes receptivity something that is valuable for planning not because it is predictable, but only because it is recognizable in a given population.[20]

The pull to make receptivity something that can be scientifically predicted, however, is still a part of the worldwide Church Growth Movement and is certainly a major

---

[18]Ibid., p. 246.

[19]Ibid., p. 257.

[20]Ibid. See the discussion following the previous quotation.

factor in the American Church Growth Movement. Wagner writes that "much research is being carried on to identify the world's distinct peoples and to gauge their present degree of receptivity to the gospel."[21] He notes that under the auspices of the Lausanne Strategy Working Group the computer bank of World Vision International is listing unreached peoples and classifying them as "very receptive, receptive, indifferent, reluctant, and very reluctant."[22] McGavran himself describes at length "common causes for fluctuation in receptivity."[23]

In American Church Growth, the same principles that McGavran applies to whole societies are applied to individuals. The question American Church Growth asks is, When can I best speak the gospel to this or that person and have my best chance of leading him or her to faith? Charles Arn says, "A well-tested principle of church growth is that unchurched people are most responsive to a change in life-style [i.e., becoming Christians and responsible church members] during *periods of transition.*"[24]

He states the implications of this for Church Growth strategy:

> Congregations . . . properly focused on outreach know that substantial ministry and growth are available when the church can establish systems to identify periods of transition in unchurched people around them, and then reach these people,

---

[21]C. Peter Wagner, *Church Growth and the Whole Gospel* (San Francisco: Harper and Row, 1981), p. 77.

[22]Ibid.

[23]McGavran, *Understanding Church Growth,* pp. 248-256.

[24]W. Charles Arn, "How to Find Receptive People," *The Pastor's Church Growth Handbook,* vol. 1, ed. Win Arn (Pasadena: Church Growth Press, 1979), p. 143.

and introduce them to the caring love of Christ and fellowship of the local church.[25]

The tool used to discover receptive people is the Holmes Stress Scale.[26] This scale lists various life changes and then rates the amount of stress each generates. The theory is that the more the stress, the more receptive a person is to the gospel. On a popular level, this is how the science of sociology is used by the American Church Growth Movement in planning who should be the focus of outreach efforts. It accounts for the intensely sociological congregational and community studies Church Growth feels are necessary before productive outreach can begin.

Lutheran and Reformed theology and science

Evangelical / Reformed theology as a science

I believe that Evangelical/Reformed theology is to a large degree compatible with a scientific approach to evangelism. The same points made previously in our discussion on vision and goals apply here. We need only review them briefly. Within the "infused grace" model of Christianity, people have within themselves the ability to apply themselves to salvation, or to make a decision to serve Christ. By nature, man wants either to become a worse sinner or to become a more moral person. In the former case he enjoys the pleasure and in the latter case he enjoys the civic blessings that God attaches to morality. Because Evangelical churches consider the purpose of the gospel to lead to morality, they are essentially working with a natural desire—hence the importance of sociology for them.

I believe this natural desire for morality is the dynamic behind the teaching of "prevenient grace," which

---

[25]Ibid., p. 143.

[26]It comes in various adaptations. See Charles Arn, op. cit., p. 144 for one example.

is a basic foundation on which Church Growth and its emphasis on receptivity is based.[27] In short, since the Evangelical is working with the desires of the natural human spirit, his work can be reduced to scientific principles and people can be rated as to their point of receptivity to the infusion of moral power.

I realize the implications of what I am saying. The Evangelical/Reformed conversion experience—*to the extent that it focuses on morality and not on justification*—is the reception of a spirit different from the Holy Spirit. I am saying that the power that the Reformed person feels to become more moral—to the extent that the power is not based on the joy of forgiveness—is a power granted by another spirit. Just as there is a difference in the definition of the gospel, so there is a different spirit. Regeneration in the Evangelical context is not true regeneration at all if it is centered on a bare desire to serve God. The infused grace that it believes comes from God is really only the power of another spirit—a spirit, we might add, that is received and maintained only by the law. Unless the true Spirit does his work of conversion using the law and the gospel, no true church growth has occurred, whether in a Lutheran congregation or in a Reformed one.[28]

---

[27]See Hunter, *The Contagious Congregation,* pp. 105,106. Hunter asks, "When people become receptive, why do they?" He answers, "A twofold explanation will give the evangelizing congregation enough knowledge to form a basis for action. First, some events and circumstances in the life of a person (or a people) open doors that stimulate an openness to new life-possibilities and permit the reception of previous screened-out messages. Second, God's Holy Spirit works through the events and circumstances of some people's lives to create receptivity, to 'warm the heart' for the Gospel. This is the Wesleyan doctrine of prevenient grace."

[28]I realize these are strong statements. The reader should understand that while attending sessions at Fuller, especially "Life and Renewal of the Church," I became aware that I had to come to a firm conclusion on the nature of this spirit. In those classes and to a certain extent in Church Growth lectures, my spirit was challenged and its validity questioned. The reader may not agree with my conclusion, but the forcefulness of the Fuller lectures have compelled me to be decisive also.

To relate this to mission work, if the Evangelical/Reformed conversion experience is a natural phenomenon, or more precisely, one brought on through a spirit that is compatible with the human spirit, then the techniques developed through the insights of human sociology are perfectly valid for predicting and effecting such a conversion. Researchers can chart this type of receptivity, for it is nothing other than the natural desire to change one's life for one reason or another. Moreover, techniques centering on felt needs will work.

In this setting, growth can be anticipated given the right circumstances; goals and visions are valid tools; the sociological needs of man are the correct places to begin; and the Church Growth Movement's scientific emphasis is truly God's gift to us in this century.

Scripture and science

The Bible writers place little or no emphasis on the use of social sciences to further the work of the church. We have seen that a bare emphasis on numbers, goals, visions, and the use of felt needs finds no support in Scripture. We find the same to be true of the use of science, in that Scripture does not consider science to be a tool to gain people for Christ.

In fact, we find just the opposite. In 2 Corinthians, Paul was writing against people whom he labeled "super-apostles" (2 Corinthians 11:5). These people seemed to have been highly trained in public speaking (11:6), and they seemed to have had the habit of speaking well about themselves (11:18). Paul's way of dealing with these people was to boast only about his "weaknesses" (11:30), for he knew that "when I am weak, then I am strong" (12:10). Only then was he depending on God's grace.

In the beginning of 1 Corinthians, Paul is adamant about his methods. He speaks against the "wise man," the "scholar," the "philosopher of this age" (1 Corinthians 1:20). Their methods did not help him. His method was to proclaim the gospel—not the gospel of infused grace, but the gospel of the forgiveness of sins won for the world on the cross. He states,

> When I came to you, brothers, I did not come with eloquence or superior wisdom as I proclaimed to you the testimony about God. For I resolved to know nothing while I was with you except Jesus Christ and him crucified. I came to you in weakness and fear, and with much trembling. (1 Corinthians 2:1-3)

His was not the confidence that came through scientific analysis, but a mixture of confidence and humility that came from knowing that people by nature reject the gospel. If anyone comes to faith, it is by God's grace alone.

In the New Testament, there is no emphasis on using tools to discover who is receptive. Nor is there any intimation that various circumstances in life make a person more or less receptive. Rather, Scripture describes the spread of the gospel of justification and does not set before us a description of the hidden workings of God on people's hearts with his law.

In other words, there is no evidence to suggest that circumstances in life that are "on the surface" and visible to us have a special role in God's leading a person to see the necessity of Christianity. Many whose lives were going along just fine from our vantage point were feeling the guilt of their sin as God worked on them, and many who you would think should be ripe for a conversion experience only hardened their hearts. Such is the case today for those who deal with the gospel of justification—while, I admit, those who work with a gospel of infused grace might find it otherwise. (See the previous discussion on the jailer at Philippi.)[29]

Lutheran theology and science

If Lutheran theology is a correct understanding of Scripture, as I believe it is, the Church Growth Movement's emphasis on science can only serve to undermine the work of the church. First, it undermines the paradox of God's grace alone by bringing into the equation a factor that balances it and makes it understandable. Second, it undermines the gospel by changing its nature, and so waters down the convert's sense of the guilt of sin and his or her appreciation of Christ's forgiveness.

The Lutheran emphasis on the gospel as God's justification of the sinner has tremendous implications for his posture toward the use of sociology. To the Lutheran, the use of the skills and insights of the world can only be a "handmaid" or "servant" of the gospel.

But what does it mean to serve as a "handmaid" of the gospel? I think it is safe to say that serving as a "handmaid" of the Evangelical/Reformed gospel is different from serving as a handmaid of the Lutheran gospel. If man's powers enter into conversion, the concept of "handmaid" cannot be fully maintained. The handmaid in that setting becomes a tool that contains a certain amount of power.

But if the gospel, as Lutherans understand it, is the only tool that God uses to convert people, how do we keep these other things in their place? How do we see to

---

[29]If one insists on a Lutheran definition of receptivity, it would have to be what Paul refers to when he writes, "God has bound all men over to disobedience so that he may have mercy on them all" (Romans 11:32). But that is not receptivity in the true sense. Paul is describing a position that people find themselves in that only becomes important when they come into contact with the gospel. It denotes no "yearning" on their part, but only a deeper sense of guilt.

it that the insights and techniques of the arts and sciences maintain the status of a handmaid for the gospel?

I believe the answer lies not in a strict classification of methods into those that are good to use and those that are dangerous to use. We have already discussed some techniques of American Church Growth that by their very definition fall out of the category of handmaid. I am sure that others who are working in other areas of the ministry such as preaching, stewardship, leadership, lay ministry, or counseling could name methods that likewise are used for the power they contain and do not serve the power of the gospel.

On the other hand, there are many things that are based on insight and techniques learned from the world that can be used in a God-pleasing way. So we ask, how can we truly maintain the power of the Word at the center of our ministry and still use methods that in the world's use of them become a power in themselves? For example, how do we preach effectively without letting good communication theory become the source of our effectiveness and so supplant the Word?

We'll find the answer partially in classification and, to a greater degree, in the attitudes and motivations derived from our theology. If the gospel is understood as the justification of sinners, the Christian will have the right understanding of grace. And if a Christian has the right understanding of grace, he will also have a spirit of humility that will depend on God to work through the message of the gospel to cause his church to grow. All Christians struggle with this problem; none of us is fully capable of walking the tightrope of keeping all his skills on the level of a handmaid. One reason for studying St. Paul, though, is to study the ways of a man who by God's grace handled this matter as well as humanly possible.

Another way of looking at the matter is to think of the diagram in chapter 10. If we keep within the sphere of activity as God has defined for us, we will be in a position both to use creatively the technology and ideas of the world and, at the same time, have a sensitivity for knowing when we are straying into a misuse of these items.

When helpful suggestions for church structure and worship that are intended to be only "handmaids" of the gospel are raised to the level of the means to excellence, the church runs the risk of losing its soul. We must keep in mind that what is in us, in a Lutheran theological context, is produced and sustained only with the law and gospel. A Lutheran commits a double error when he copies the ministry of the Evangelical. First, he copies the mechanics of another's ministry and so does not allow what is in himself to dictate his methods. Second, he copies the Evangelical's expression of what is in him—namely, the spirit of infused grace—and so stifles the Spirit of forgiveness that wants to express himself through the Lutheran in other ways.

Some ask, "But aren't there good ideas we can learn from Church Growth?" Then they go on to give examples such as having adequate parking and good property maintenance. The Church Growth Movement itself gives only marginal reference to these common sense sort of things. The movement itself acknowledges that such suggestions are nothing new. The real issue is that Church Growth makes the growth of the church a science and so elevates sociological help to the level of a power for growth.[30] It is not common sense suggestions that I object to. Rather, it is the Evangelical/Reformed theology which, as I have argued, rejects the gospel as the means of grace and infuses a heavy dose of sociology into the conversion process itself.

---

[30]Note again Peter Wagner's statement, "Church growth looks to social science as a cognate discipline." Wagner, *Church Growth: State of the Art,* p. 33.

There are those who argue, "The Lord operates within the sphere of human psychology when he converts, so we must not be shy about learning psychological principles." Once again, this sort of talk only throws a smoke screen around the real issue. The issue is not whether the Lord operates within the sphere of our heart, mind, and body—our "psychology" if you will—but that the agent he uses within us is the gospel. A minister must understand the dynamics of the law and gospel working on the sinful canvas of our psychology (a sinfulness that psychology usually will not recognize). An understanding and ability to work with this dynamic cannot be gained from learning about psychology. It can only be learned by working with God's Word, witnessing how it works on people, and learning how to be spiritual leaders from the example of Jesus and the apostles.

I would be less than honest if I said I have not implemented any insights from Church Growth into my ministry. I will continue to hold on to some of those ideas. While studying Church Growth, however, I also felt the siren song of success through sociological principles. As I read about those principles I noticed myself developing a different attitude toward my ministry. The desire to serve people with the Word of God and to find my answers from the Bible subtly began to wane. It became more fun to search for answers in Church Growth books, for they promised me a scientific answer—something I could get my hands on.

Even though I knew what Church Growth was like before I entered the Fuller program, the assigned reading that I had planned to do as an academic exercise began to become almost like a drug. I realize better now that theologically we are what we read. Correct reading of Church Growth and similar literature is much more than simply excising a few paragraphs on decision theology or ignoring digs at baptismal regeneration. The reader is dealing with a shift in emphasis where the right thing might be said but in the wrong context or where the author places psychology and sociology in a much different relation to the gospel than does the reader. The reader is dealing with a different spirit, and while stones can be filtered out by a screen, the wind cannot. In my mind the risks for a confessional Lutheran using the Church Growth library are greater than the benefits, in spite of some good practical suggestions that may be found there.

I think that confessional Lutherans should develop and teach their own pastoral theology in the realm of evangelism and depend more on the wealth of experience within their own circles. We may gain good practical suggestions from Church Growth type literature, but we will be time ahead if we stick to the Bible and pray that the Lord will give us wisdom to apply its truths to our ministry.

I have not given a rigid answer to those looking for clear direction on letting their skills remain on the level of a handmaid to the gospel. We should realize, though, that the proper and improper use of the methods of the world "touch" at a point sometimes difficult for us to see. Those who understand the nature of the gospel and who stray into the improper use of their skills and technology will soon catch themselves and move back into a proper use of them. Those who don't understand the gospel as the forgiveness of sin, or who are unclear in their understanding, will find themselves straying far into the improper use.

God calls us to preach the gospel of justification and to pray that the Lord will always keep our hearts humbly trusting in the gospel alone to bring people into his family. Having done that, we will find ourselves with the wisdom necessary for deciding whether or not to use what the world has to offer. I might add that a good indicator of where a person stands is how much he is willing to agree that the Bible contains *everything* he needs to know about the dynamics of his faith and the performance of his ministry (2 Timothy 3:16). Those who jump on that statement and immediately list all the wonderful benefits science and technology have given the church perhaps have missed the point.

Another way of looking at the issue is that the gospel creates its own sociology. Christians must realize that they are not trying to build a human organization. While the people in the church are human and are governed by the sociological rules that all humans find themselves under, our purpose is to present the gospel that will bring people from darkness to light and enable them to love God and their neighbor. The gospel alone creates love, and love alone creates a "sociology" that makes everything in a congregation pleasing to God.

We must abandon the notion that to be successful we must use the sociological structures of the world. We need to realize that the church is called to do the most sociologically foolish thing anyone can do: tell a person he is a sinner and condemned by God and then tell him to put his hope in Christ who died on a cross to erase his guilt. That message is foolishness to those who are perishing. It is also sociologically foolish to many in the Church Growth Movement who claim that to be effective we should not be negative in the pulpit.

We must hold firmly to the fact that only the law points out sin and only the gospel elicits faith and leads a sinner to know that he is forgiven. And only when this happens can a person understand true "sociology." For only then does he begin to love and be part of a body of people who are "sociologically" pleasing to God.

The back-door loss analysis that has been so popular in recent years must never be done with the attitude that there are two dynamics working in the congregation—one sociological and the other spiritual. That would be the same as compartmentalizing our lives into spiritual and secular areas. We must realize that for every "sociological" offense a spiritual reason can be found, either on the part of the congregation or on the part of the one offended. That is, a congregation's sociological problems are really spiritual problems. Attempting to deal with the issue on a sociological basis reduces the work of the church to the level of a secular organization. It misses the point that the church must deal with people as "new creations," who can only be rebuked, encouraged, and motivated by the law and the gospel. We should focus on the spiritual nature of the problem and its spiritual answer. Working through the problem from that standpoint, the sociological problem will disappear or become a moot point.

A good illustration of this is Paul's words to the Corinthians, a congregation that was doing everything "sociologically" wrong. When Paul heard that they were showing favoritism and treating the poor in a despicable way—right in the middle of the dinner in which they shared the Lord's body and blood—he did not order a change in congregational organization or structure. He told them bluntly, "Your meetings do more harm than good" (1 Corinthians 11:17). Then he reminded them of what the Lord's Supper meant for them and how in that Supper they received the body and blood of Christ who in love had died and risen for them. Paul was confident that the law and gospel would lead the Corinthians to change their attitude toward the poor Christians among them. That changed attitude would find the "structures" necessary to see to it that all were treated in a loving way.

Application

In my ministry I will want to remain as current as I can in all the tools available for studying the Word and presenting it to others. Our modern world is a treasure house of electronic tools to broadcast the Word, and we can use the printed word as never before. By God's grace, the knowledge of this world (science) can contribute much to our ability to extend the spread of the Word.

At the same time, I do not want to tap into science in any way that makes it a power for conversion and forces it out of its position as the handmaid of the gospel. I will put my confidence in what Paul tells Timothy—namely, that the Bible contains everything I need to be a fruitful Christian, which in my case includes being a pastor (2 Timothy 3:16,17).

There is a proper balance in all of this. If anyone says that the balance is easy to arrive at and maintain, he is fooling himself. We will probably all err in one direction or the other. If that is true, I would rather find myself erring toward an over dependence on Scripture. If I err in that direction, I will be closer to the Lord who can jolt me in the right course and lead me to find help from my fellow workers! But if I err in the other way—as I found myself doing—I'm not as sure the strength will always be there to return to a dependence on Scripture.

A few minutes on our knees in prayer, asking God to bless the preaching of the law and gospel, is worth more than hours trying to discover a human point of contact. An hour reading the Bible gives us more true zeal than a hundred hours of reading about the findings of sociology. An ounce of the Spirit of God is worth more than a gallon of technique. Technique is important, but real technique comes from keeping our eyes on the kingdom of God. It comes from knowing that the Spirit of God will give us ministerial skill and ability. He alone knows the right way to spread the gospel.

15.

REACTIONS AND OUTCOMES

Reactions to Church Growth

The Church Growth Movement has come under much criticism from various sources. This book also has leveled some criticism against it. It might be helpful to look briefly at other criticisms of the movement so that the reader will be able to view this book in a wider context.

The liberal reaction

As those who are concerned with social service and social action, the liberal churches have reacted to the Church Growth Movement as a classist movement. Their emphasis on social reconciliation of all people constrains them to object to McGavran's homogeneous unit principle.[1] Their concerns also lead them to object

---

[1]For a discussion of the homogeneous unit debate, see C. Peter Wagner, *Our Kind of People* (Atlanta: John Knox Press, 1979), pp. 8-33, especially p. 23.

to Church Growth emphasis on conversion, a criticism they level at evangelical churches in general.[2] With their open view of all religions, liberal churches deplore those who teach that Christ is the only way of salvation, and they view the planting of Christian churches as an intrusion on the religion and culture of other peoples.[3]

These objections are not my objections. I firmly believe that conversion is the Lord's work, that Christ is the only way of salvation, and that it is the duty of the church to attempt to extend the influence of the gospel through preaching and teaching—which will result in the Lord forming new congregations of believers.

The Evangelical reaction

Many Evangelicals and neo-Evangelicals have bought into Church Growth. There are, however, objectors to Church Growth among Evangelicals. (Fundamentalists are often against Church Growth but I will not be addressing their writings.) For example, in his book, *Church Growth: A Mighty River,* Delos Miles includes a chapter entitled, "It's Possible Pollution." According to Miles, possible sources of pollution include its faulty hermeneutics,[4] its weak theological base, and its pragmatic attitude.[5]

Arthur Johnston has expressed concerns about the sociological emphases of Church Growth. He states:

---

[2]C. Peter Wagner, *Church Growth and the Whole Gospel* (San Francisco: Harper and Row, 1981), p. 3.

[3]The issue of Church Growth polemics is discussed by Charles Van Engen in *The Growth of the True Church* (Amsterdam: Rodopi, 1981), pp. 19ff.

[4]Delos Miles, *Church Growth: A Mighty River* (Nashville: Broadman, 1981), pp. 134,135. His main objection, which this author shares, is that Church Growth reads cultural issues into Scripture where it is questionable at best that such issues were on the minds of the authors.

[5]Ibid., pp. 138-141.

It seems to me there is a problem when one is depending on the dynamic of social change as the barometer of the responsiveness of a people to Christ. It has been looked at as sociological and psychological. The vacuum can be filled by Christ. This is true if there has been real conversion to Christ. . . . Sometimes [however] the people movement will deal superficially with the culture. . . . In [such] group movements, it can lead to group reversions and to syncretism.

History suggests, I believe, that when Christian proclamation does not adapt to culture but demands total change and makes the decision very hard, sometimes entailing even martyrdom, the result is that belief becomes deep-rooted, and deviation is less when winds of social change come along later.[6]

Others have expressed frustration caused by the high-powered emphasis on numbers and sociological expertise. One Baptist minister wrote, "The use of numerical growth as the standard of expectation and evaluation also affects our self-image. When numerical growth is not realized we often conclude that our professional ability is below standard. It is a frustrating experience and leads to self doubt."[7]

The objections that come from these sources are closer to my line of argumentation. But they do not really get

---

[6]Arthur Johnston and C. Peter Wagner, "Intensity of Belief: A Pragmatic Concern for Church Growth," *Christianity Today* (January 7, 1977): 10-14. This is a transcript of a discussion with Peter Wagner. For a full discussion of Johnston's arguments, as well as an excellent overview of the course of Evangelical missiology in the last hundred years, see Arthur Johnston, *The Battle for World Evangelism* (Wheaton, Ill.: Tyndale, 1978).

[7]David W. Andersen, "What Was Your Average Attendance Last Year?" *Your Church* (January/February 1983), pp. 20-23.

at the main issue. Because they are in the evangelical camp, they themselves hold a theology that I believe is at the heart of why Church Growth errs as it does. For that reason they are not able to see the root of the problem.

Lutheran Church—Missouri Synod reactions

While many in the LCMS have fully accepted the Church Growth program, there are many in the synod who have expressed objections. The "official" stance of the Synod is one of caution.

In 1987 the "Commission on Theology and Church Relations" published a pamphlet that analyzed the Church Growth Movement. In the final chapter they offer evaluation and recommendations. The first recommendation is, "Missiological principles must be applied in a way that correctly distinguishes between law and gospel."[8] This concern is at the heart of my analysis also. They also express concerns over the use of sociological "soil testing" to find communities that are receptive to the gospel. While they admit that the "Holy Spirit does at times use events in the life of unconverted people to prepare them for the gospel," they explain that "such crises are applications of the law [that] cause the person to become aware of the fact that he or she has sinned against God, deserves His wrath and punishment." But "in the strict sense, the individual stops resisting and becomes receptive to the gospel only at the time of conversion."[9]

Concerning the use of sociological principles to build the church, they rightly say, "If Lutherans use Church Growth materials, they must realize that the means of grace and mission methods serve different functions and purposes. Only the means of grace truly build the church.

---

[8]Commission on Theology and Church Relations of The Lutheran Church —Missouri Synod, *Evangelism and Church Growth* (1987), p. 37.

[9]Ibid., p. 38.

Organization is clearly not a means of grace and therefore does not itself build the church or cause it to grow."[10]

They add that these principles "with Biblically tested criteria"[11] can be used as a handmaid of the gospel: "To be sure, there is a sense in which it can serve the gospel."[12]

These statements by the Missouri Synod deserve to be read by all of their members. The Missouri Synod has the background and theological understanding to analyze the issues Church Growth has raised. But considering that many of their members are buying into the Church Growth methodology without doing serious theological work, it remains to be seen whether their theological discernment can be maintained.

The theological outcome for Church Growth adherents

As stated previously, this book was not meant to be a polemic against Church Growth. Rather, it was to address various issues raised by the Church Growth Movement and analyze them in the light of Scripture. My reference to the Church Growth Movement implies nothing personal against that movement. If anything, it shows my appreciation for the tremendous influence of the movement, as well as the fact that within the movement all the major issues that face pastors today have come to the surface and been discussed.

Keeping in mind that we are focusing on the issues and not on individuals, we will use the Church Growth Movement to teach us one more lesson. We will take a look at where Church Growth ideas eventually lead an adherent.

---

[10]Ibid., p. 41.

[11]Ibid., p. 50.

[12]Ibid., p. 41.

To do this, we will use the picture introduced in chapter ten. The diagram shows that the trouble with Church Growth theology is that it moves outside the sphere of responsibility God has given to the church. In doing so, it finds itself with a deficient methodology.

In reacting against the liberals of their day who were doing less than they should, Donald McGavran and his followers chose a course of action in which they felt constrained to carry a heavier burden and wider range of responsibilities than God expected of them. In believing that God had given them the responsibility to grow numerically, they plugged themselves into a mindset that ultimately moved the "peg" from the job of teaching to the actual attainment of results.

Having taken a posture of being "higher up" in the work of God than those who consider it their duty simply to preach the word, Church Growth finds itself using a "higher" brand of methodology. It finds itself using human powers in a "higher" way than those who center on justification and believe in God's grace alone. We can identify three of these "higher" positions.

First, there is the higher use of sociology. Sociology becomes at least part of the power behind the growth of the church. One of the purposes of this book has been to show the danger of such a higher use of sociology.

The second "higher" involves a higher use of reason. The "higher" use of reason takes place in sociology to be sure, but here I mean the higher use of reason in the interpretation of Scripture. Just how the Church Growth Movement stands on interpreting Scripture has become clearer as time goes on. Donald McGavran has stated that he had a high view of Scripture. Miles Delos quotes McGavran on this point, "God used a current language and a current culture, but was not bound or limited by them. The writers, while immersed in their cultures, were inspired and therefore not culture bound."[13]

More recently, Peter Wagner has described his hermeneutics. His hermeneutics are in line with those of Fuller Seminary, which generally has adopted a form of the historical-critical method of interpreting the Bible.[14] Wagner discusses the hermeneutics of the homogeneous unit theory.

> The Bible is inert in the sense that what it describes was actually said and actually happened, because God made sure that the men who inscribed his revelation did so accurately. . . . However, those who wrote the Scriptures used language, thought forms, proverbs, idioms, and cultural assumptions that made what they wrote perfectly intelligible *at face value* in only one cultural setting at one point in history. Attempts to understand Scripture by people of any other culture at any other time need a special effort of interpretation that the original receptors took for granted.

> . . . A full understanding of the absolute principles in the Bible cannot come apart from an understanding of the precise historical situations in which they were given. As context is more adequately understood, the supracultural content of revelation becomes clearer.

> What is the supracultural content of Scripture? A great deal of caution must be exercised in an-

---

[13]Donald McGavran, *The Clash Between Christianity and Cultures* (Washington, D.C.: Canon Press, 1974), p. 53, quoted in Delos Miles, op. cit., pp. 136,137.

[14]For a discussion of Fuller's hermeneutics, see the chapter entitled "The Strange Case of Fuller Theological Seminary," in Harold Lindsell, *The Battle for the Bible* (Grand Rapids: Zondervan, 1976), pp. 106-121.

swering this important question. All attempts to reduce the supracultural content of revelation to a creed will naturally be colored by the cultural context in which the creed is formulated.

. . . Nevertheless there are certain concepts that emerge from Scripture that probably would be universally recognized as supracultural principles of Christianity: Truth, justice, love, sin, the existence of God, faith, forgiveness, prayer, honesty, marriage, the historicity of Jesus, . . . But as words, they are so abstract that they have very little intrinsic meaning. The practical meaning of each of these concepts can only emerge in a historical and cultural context.

. . . Such an approach to theological reflection does require a measure of humility that some people might not be able to accept. However, it clears the way for theology to become theologies, reduces the possibility of a dominant group of Christians becoming theologically chauvinistic, and allows for a full and free working of the Spirit of God among diverse peoples in a pluralistic society.[15]

From this quotation, we can see that Wagner's hermeneutic is not centered on forgiveness, and is strongly influenced by his sociological mindset. To him, the gospel contains the message of forgiveness, but forgiveness is only one blessing among many and is so relativized by Wagner as to make it inconsequential. The point we wish to make from this quotation, though, is that Wagner's method of interpreting Scripture is definitely "historical-critical." In this method, man's reason

---

[15]Wagner, *Our Kind of People,* pp. 88,89.

takes a "higher" place—putting itself over Scripture. Man's reason claims to be the judge of Scripture, and thus only someone properly versed in the social sciences can judge what the Bible says to us today.

The next "higher" position that Church Growth leads to is in the area of spirituality. The intensely pragmatic nature of Church Growth has led it to adopt the charismatic spirit in view of the fast growth of charismatic churches throughout the world. I direct the reader to Wagner's *Spiritual Power and Church Growth* for a full discussion of Church Growth's charismatic position.[16] In my opinion, the charismatic spirit is not the true Spirit. Rather, it is a "higher" spirit, one that is bound up with the law and not the gospel. It feels good—which is why it is so appealing. It springs from a desire for a "higher spirituality" and a "higher morality," rather than from the message of forgiveness spoken to a troubled conscience.

These facets of the Church Growth Movement are all pieces of a whole complex that moves beyond the responsibility God has assigned to his disciples. They begin with a human desire for morality in the face of the demands of the law, rather than with a humble contrition over sins committed. Any church body that incorporates one of these "higher" facets into its theology or methodology will soon find itself using the rest.

Tragically, such "higher" facets end with using the law as a way to peace with God. They supplant the Christian's trust in Christ's forgiveness alone for his peace.

Where do we go from here?

My aim in this book has been to preserve the message of forgiveness as the heart of our faith, and so maintain a base from which we can truly serve our God with sanc-

---

[16]C. Peter Wagner, *Spiritual Power and Church Growth* (Altamonte Springs, Fla.: Strang Communications, 1986).

tified lives. Anyone who thinks the arguments presented in this book arise from a spirit that cares little for sanctification has not understood the points I have made. In part, this entire study has come out of my desire to know why I should live a moral life. The world and some churches give a flood of reasons for serving God, reasons having to do with health, well-being, and spiritual peace. But such reasons are based on gilded selfish human ambition.

For me, there is only one reason why I should live a moral life. That is because the Lord who loves me and died for me wants me to. It matters little to me what benefits I accrue from an increase in sanctification, although I rejoice when I experience those blessings. The only thing that really matters, though, is how the Lord feels about my life. My personal experience is that growth in faith and sanctification—which I admit has a long way to go—comes only when I remember my sins and what they deserve, and then think about the fact that I am forgiven. I live knowing what would happen if I were to die as a slave to sin and as one who rejected the grace of God.

What is at issue is not sanctification versus justification, but an Evangelical/Reformed understanding of the gospel versus a Lutheran understanding. The Bible clearly states that God has created for himself a new people, "eager to do what is good" (Titus 2:14).

The entire argument in this book is that only the gospel as a message of forgiveness can bestow both eternal life and a life lived now in service to God. Only the Lutheran understanding of justification can lead to a life of service that is lived *for God* and for him alone. All other definitions of justification result in a type of sanctification that is produced to gain something for the doer.

This book has not been written with an unrealistic view of the way people are. All of us get confused as to why we do what we do. Often, our motivation for living the "Christian" life is not simply the love of Christ. This fact should spur pastors and teachers on to leading our people to appreciate their Savior more and to live lives that are motivated for the right reasons.

Granted, God attaches blessing to keeping his law. For a Christian these blessings are one reason for him to keep the law. He views these blessings as rewards of grace, given by God to encourage him to continue in his struggle of faith. But a Christian who understands the centrality of God's forgiveness will not consider those blessings the main goal of his Christianity. Such an abuse becomes a real possibility, though, when an evangelist plays to the natural desires of the unbeliever and uses rewards as the incentive to become a Christian, or even as an incentive to come into a place where the gospel message is presented. An unbeliever cannot understand the rewards God promises his people for lives of service to him, until that unbeliever becomes one of God's own through repentance and faith.

A church can continue to grow in service to God only when it abandons its desire to be sanctified per se, and focuses more on the love of God that is ours through the Savior. Whenever the church focuses on numerical growth, or sanctification, or renewal, or on any of the by-products of the gospel, it runs the danger of losing the very treasures it is striving to keep. Whenever it uses methods that tap into a person's natural desire to reap the benefits of a moral life, it jeopardizes its chance of reaching that person with the real gospel and may inoculate him against real Christianity for the rest of his life. The blessings attached to morality will continue to be an incentive for the unbelieving world to live according to the commandments. But a church is wrong to use that motive as a deliberate evangelism tool.

A church body should not allow the natural pull of mankind for a more moral or happier life to dictate the direction of its evangelism work or of its ministry in general. Our goal is salvation from the guilt of sin—that is, the punishment we would have received because of our sins—and from death and hell. Our goal is salvation from the dead works of the law to living works done out of love for God.

Everything we do should be done with a view to God's final act of salvation—giving his people their inheritance in the new heaven and the new earth. Our calling is to preach the law that condemns people and the gospel that saves them from the guilt of sin and eternal punishment and then urge them to live God-pleasing lives. When we do this, we can eagerly look forward to God's giving us numerical growth, sanctification, and renewal. We can rejoice when we find ourselves being led into a fuller service to God. This kind of growth may not be as quick as we like, and it may not bring us the earthly blessings we had hoped for. But it does bring real joy, and God is glorified.

The key lies in Jesus' words, "Seek first [God's] kingdom and his righteousness, and all these things will be given to you as well" (Matthew 6:33). Our God is not stingy with his blessings. The Christian *can* look forward to a life filled with God's blessings in this world. The trick is to maintain a balance whereby we are not always keeping one eye on the blessings God promises to give us in life.

When we find ourselves "using the gospel" to effect items on our own human agendas, we will find ourselves slowly losing the very thing we hope to preserve. Only contrition and faith in God's forgiveness enable us to keep it all straight. The Evangelical/Reformed gospel and the methods that flow from it invariably downplay the centrality of forgiveness and keep a person from seeking

219

the kingdom of God as Scripture uses that term. They lead to a conversion experience that is saturated with promises about what God will achieve for the person who takes Christ into his life. And if those promises are not completely fulfilled according to the believer's expectations, then God's grace ceases to be full and complete.

What's more, they lead to a religion where the means of grace are downplayed, since man's efforts to some extent become his means of grace. The paradox of grace is broken and man is left to himself to work his way into God's favor—or wonder whether God's favor is really intended for him.

Lutherans have received the most wonderful heritage any church can possess. We have been given the undeserved privilege to live under Christ in the shadow of a man who understood God's gift of forgiveness as no man has since the days of the Apostles. Through Luther, we have been led to appreciate that all areas of theology center on justification.

It is my opinion that the Lutheran Church is in the best position to examine how the gospel should be spread. It is a shame when we don't do it as we should. It is a double shame when we listen to the siren song of methods that flow from religious bodies whose understanding of the gospel and the kingdom of God is less than complete and who ultimately have the potential of leading people back under the law.

We err when we expect to find surefire methods somewhere out there. When Lutherans get together to discuss methods, we should begin with the understanding that we must lead people to an awareness of guilt over their sins, so that the gospel can do its saving work. We should begin with the recognition that there is a paradox of grace we must work with. Moreover, the Holy Spirit works when and where he wills, and we cannot predict or shape this work.

If at times it seems we are not able to match the flashy and interesting methods of the Evangelical/Reformed, we should not feel too discouraged. We ought not think that since our message is more biblical, we should be able to outdistance others in the appeal of our methods. The nature of the gospel limits us to the work of preaching and teaching at church and in people's homes, among our members and with prospects. We should come away from methodology brainstorming sessions with a great sense of solidarity with those who have gone before. Our forebears relied on the Spirit to make them effective, by giving them courage to speak clearly the message of grace in the many opportunities God placed in their path.

In the end, we'll find that the answer is not so much in methods as in the Word we preach. To those who begin their work with a clear definition of the gospel, the Lord will give wisdom to develop appropriate methods to serve as vehicles for that gospel. If this book has encouraged any discussion to this end, it will have served its purpose.

Appendix A

QUESTIONS FOR DISCUSSION

These questions are examples of the specific questions I believe church leaders should be asking themselves. They are arranged in the order of the chapters in this book.

A. *Visions and goals*

1. How exactly do we define the term "vision" in the light of the present charismatic movement's definition, a definition that is shared by the Church Growth Movement?

2. In what sense does one depend on the inherent power of a vision to impel one forward in a project? What is the relation of the power of a vision to the power of the gospel? Have we adequately described to ourselves the role that each should play in our ministry?

3. When does a goal enter into the sphere of activity the Holy Spirit has left for himself?
4. Which goals are legitimate and which are not? Is it legitimate to set the number of souls we want our church to have by a certain date? Is it legitimate to determine the number of evangelism calls we wish to make? Is it legitimate to determine the number of flyers we wish to distribute, ads we wish to make, homes we wish to canvass?

B. *The desire to grow*

1. Is there an antithesis between the desire for numbers and the desire to spread the gospel?
2. Have I adequately applied the teaching of God's election to my evangelism efforts?

C. *Felt needs*

1. Have I defined for myself the difference between the classic felt needs approach of the Church Growth Movement, and the point of contact approach suggested in this book?
2. Have I carefully analyzed whether a program I am using is (a) correctly designed to lead a person into the gospel of God's forgiveness or (b) inadvertently giving a person a reason for misunderstanding why my church is here?

D. *Church growth as a science*

1. Have I adequately defined for myself what it means to be effective in the ministry?
2. Have I adequately applied the teaching of the Christian as saint and sinner to my appraisal of how an ideal church should look?
3. To what extent have I wrestled with the hermeneutical question regarding the sufficiency of

Scripture, not only in the realm of determining theology and morals, but also in the realm of determining evangelism methods? What role do the descriptive sections of Scripture have as models for our evangelism work today?

4. What exactly are the social sciences? What are some of their basic premises? What is its underlying view of man? If we choose to use the insights of the social sciences, what specific principles are we using to filter out a possible wrong view of man?

5. What specifically is lacking in Scripture that the social sciences can supply?

Appendix B

THE NATURE OF CONVERSION

Lutheran	**Reformed**
What precipitates conversion	
Through the law the Holy Spirit leads people to know that they are sinners. They experience fear of God and uncertainty about their eternity.	A person is led to yearn for the power to live a better life. The reason for this yearning varies. It might be a desire to live better so as to be more at peace with God. It might he the desire to overcome the bad effects of sin on one's life. It may be a desire to remove the harmful effects of sin in society. The preaching of the law always takes the characteristic of pointing out the problems that sin causes and the relief that Christianity will give.

Lutheran	Reformed
What people are told to do	
People are told to believe the fact that Christ has died on the cross for their sins and to rest in his gracious pardon. They are warned that "doing" anything themselves will only get in the way of God's forgiveness.	People are told to yield themselves to the pull of God's Spirit and that if they open themselves to him he will enter and give them his blessings—the power to live godly lives and pardon for all sins. Often a "law" passage is the catalyst for conversion rather than a "gospel" passage.
What it brings about	
It brings peace with God and a desire to live a God-pleasing life. Appreciation for the power to serve God is central to this type of conversion.	It leads a person to have a renewed desire to serve God. It brings the realization that we are to live holy lives because in Christ we have become holy in God's eyes.
The feelings associated with the conversion	
Totally dependent on the person's personality as to how one feels about his or her forgiveness. However, it is always characterized by an appreciation of the Word and sacraments—the objective means through which God brings his forgiveness.	Often carefully defined by the individual congregation, ranging from a quiet acceptance to a heavy emphasis on subjective emotional activity. Normally characterized by a well defined "I found it" experience.

227

BIBLIOGRAPHY

Works Cited

Andersen, David W. "What Was Your Average Attendance Last Year?" *Your Church* (January/February, 1983): 20-23.

Arn, Win, and Arn, Charles. *The Master's Plan for Making Disciples.* Pasadena: Church Growth Press, 1982.

Arn, Win, ed. *The Pastor's Church Growth Handbook,* Vol. 1. Pasadena: Church Growth Press, 1979.

_____ . *The Pastor's Church Growth Handbook,* Vol. 2. Pasadena: Church Growth Press, 1982.

Arn, Win. "How to Increase Your Worship and Giving by 10% or More." *The Win Arn Church Growth Report* (Number 25).

Augustine. *The Confessions of Saint Augustine.* Translated by Rex Warner. New York: New American Library, 1963.

Ayling, Stanley. *John Wesley.* New York: William Collins, 1979.

Bainton, Roland. *Here I Stand.* Nashville: Abingdon, 1950.

Bales, Harold D. *A Comprehensive Plan for Evangelism.* Nashville: Discipleship Resources, 1978.

Ballard, Paul. "The Question of Church Growth." *The Baptist Quarterly,* Vol. 28 (October, 1980): 361-372.

Becker, Siegbert W. *The Foolishness of God.* Milwaukee: Northwestern Publishing House, 1982.

_____ . "Romans 1-3,9." Transcribed from audio tapes by Rev. Gerhold Lemke, 2109 Baldwin St., Sturgis, SD.

Bloesch, Donald G. *Essentials of Evangelical Theology.* New York: Harper and Row, 1979.

Calvin, John. *Commentary on the Book of the Prophet Isaiah.* Translated by William Pringle. Grand Rapids: Eerdmans, 1948.

_____ . *Institutes of the Christian Religion.* The Library of Christian Classics, Nos. 20, 21. Philadelphia: Westminster, 1960.

Carter, Charles W. ed. *A Contemporary Wesleyan Theology*, Vol. 1. Grand Rapids: Zondervan, 1983.

Chaney, Charles L., and Lewis, Ron. *Design for Church Growth.* Nashville: Broadman, 1977.

Chemnitz, Martin. *Examination of the Council of Trent.* Translated by Fred Kramer. St. Louis: Concordia, 1971.

_____. *Loci Theologici*, Vol. 1. Translated by J. A. O. Preus. Saint Louis: Concordia, 1989.

Cho, Paul Y. *More Than Numbers.* Waco: Word, 1984.

Clouse, Robert, ed. *The Meaning of the Millennium.* Downer's Grove, Intervarsity Press, 1977.

"Commission on Theology and Church Relations of the Lutheran Church—Missouri Synod." *Evangelism and Church Growth with Special Reference to the Church Growth Movement.* September, 1987.

Conn, Harvey, ed. *Theological Perspectives on Church Growth.* Phillipsburg, NJ: Presbyterian and Reformed Publishing Co., 1976.

Dodd, C. H. *The Parables of the Kingdom.* London: Nisbet, 1936.

Elliot, Ralph C. *Church Growth That Counts.* Valley Forge: Judson Press, 1982.

Erb, Peter, ed. *Pietists, Selected Writings.* New York: Paulist Press, 1983.

Erickson, Millard J. *Christian Theology.* Grand Rapids: Baker, 1984.

Fuller Theological Seminary. Class Notes for Doctor of Ministry Program. Various Sessions 1986-1987.

Gibbs, Eddie. *I Believe in Church Growth.* Grand Rapids: Eerdmans, 1981.

Hamann, Henry P. A. "Justification by Faith in Modern Theology." Th.D. Dissertation, Concordia Theological Seminary, 1956.Henry, Carl F. H., ed. *Christian Faith and Modern Theology.* New York: Channel Press, 1964.

Hesselgrave, David J. *Planting Churches Cross-Culturally: A Guide for Home and Foreign Missions.* Grand Rapids: Baker Book House, 1980.

Hunter, George G. III. *The Contagious Congregation.* Nashville: Abingdon, 1979.

Hunter, Kent R. *Foundations for Church Growth.* New Haven, Missouri: Leader Publishing Company, 1983.

Johnston, Arthur, and Wagner, C. Peter. "Intensity of Belief: A Pragmatic Concern for Church Growth." *Christianity Today.* (January 7, 1977): 10-14.

Johnston, Arthur P. *The Battle for World Evangelism.* Wheaton: Tyndale, 1978.

Kerr, Hugh T., and Mulder, John M., eds. *Conversions*. Grand Rapids: Eerdmans, 1983.

Ladd, George. *Jesus and the Kingdom*. Waco: Word Books, 1964.

Leaver, Robin A. *Luther on Justification*. Saint Louis: Concordia, 1975.

Lindsell, Harold. *The Battle for the Bible*. Grand Rapids: Zondervan, 1976.

Luecke, David S. *Evangelical Style and Lutheran Substance*. Saint Louis: Concordia, 1988.

Luther, *Martin. Luther's Works*. Edited by Jaroslav Pelikan. Vol. 2: Lectures on Genesis, Chapters 6-14, Saint Louis: Concordia, 1960.

_____ . *Luther's Works*. Edited by Jaroslav Pelikan. Vol. 5: Lectures on Genesis, Chapters 36-30. Saint Louis: Concordia, 1968.

_____ . *Luther's Works*. Edited by Jaroslav Pelikan. Vol. 7: Lectures on Genesis, Chapters 38-44. Saint Louis: Concordia, 1965.

_____ . *Luther's Works*. Edited by Jaroslav Pelikan. Vol. 8: Lectures on Genesis, Chapters 45-50. Saint Louis: Concordia, 1966.

_____ . *Luther's Works*. Edited by Jaroslav Pelikan. Vol. 12: Selected Psalms I. Saint Louis: Concordia, 1955.

_____ . *Luther's Works*. Edited by Jaroslav Pelikan. Vol. 23: Sermons on the Gospel of Saint John, Chapters 6-8. Saint Louis: Concordia, 1959.

_____ . "The Large Catechism" in *The Concordia Triglotta*. Saint Louis: Concordia, 1921.

McGavran, Donald A. *How to Grow a Church*. Ventura, California: Regal, 1973.

_____ . *Ten Steps for Church Growth*. San Francisco: Harper and Row, 1977.

_____ . *How Churches Grow*. New York: Friendship Press, 1966.

_____ . *The Bridges of God*. The United Kingdom: World Dominion Press, 1955.

_____ . *Understanding Church Growth*. Grand Rapids: Eerdmans, 1980.

McGavran, Donald, and Hunter, George. *Church Growth: Strategies That Work*. Nashville: Abingdon, 1960.

McGavran, Donald A., and Arn, Win. *Back to Basics in Church Growth*. Wheaton: Tyndale, 1981.

McGrath, Alister E. *Iustitia Dei*. 2 vols. Cambridge: Cambridge University Press, 1986.

Meyer, John P. *Ministers of Christ*. Milwaukee: Northwestern Publishing House, 1963.

Miles, Delos. *Church Growth: A Mighty River.* Nashville: Broadman Press, 1981.

Niesel, Wilhelm. *The Gospel and the Churches.* Philadelphia: Westminster, 1962.

Peters, George. *A Theology of Church Growth.* Grand Rapids: Zondervan, 1981.

Peterson, J. Randall. "Church Growth," *Christianity Today* (March 27, 1981): 18-23.

Peterson, Lorman. "The Nature of Justification," *Christian Faith and Modern Theology.* Edited by Carl F. H. Henry. New York: Channel Press (1964): 348-370.

Pieper, August. *Isaiah II.* Translated by Erwin Kowalke. Milwaukee: Northwestern Publishing House, 1979.

Pieper, Francis. *Christian Dogmatics,* 4 vols. Translated by Theodore Engelder and John Mueller. Saint Louis: Concordia, 1950.

Plass, Ewald. *What Luther Says,* 3 vols. Saint Louis: Concordia, 1959.

Preus, Klemet. "Contemporary Christian Music: An Evaluation." *Concordia Theological Quarterly,* Vol. 51 (January 1987): 1-18.

Quebedeaux, Richard. *The Young Evangelicals.* New York: Harper and Row, 1974. Here's Life Publishers, 1984.

Sasse, Hermann. *Here We Stand.* Translated by Theodore Tappert. Saint Louis: Concordia, 1966.

Senkbeil, Harold L. *Sanctification: Christ in Action.* Milwaukee: Northwestern Publishing House, 1989.

Shenk, Wilbert R., ed. *Exploring Church Growth.* Grand Rapids: Eerdmans, 1983.

Stumme, Wayne. "A Lutheran Critique of the Church Growth Movement." A taped lecture from the 1988 Lutheran Exegetical Theology Symposium at Concordia Seminary, Fort Wayne, Indiana.

The Lutheran Hymnal. Saint Louis: Concordia, 1941.

Van Engen, Charles. *The Growth of the True Church.* Amsterdam: Rodopi, 1981.

Wagner, C. Peter, ed. *Church Growth: State of the Art.* Wheaton, Illinois: Tyndale, 1986.

Wagner, C. Peter. *Church Growth and the Whole Gospel: A Biblical Mandate.* San Francisco: Harper and Row, 1981.

————. *Leading Your Church to Growth.* Ventura, California: Regal Books, 1984.

————. *On the Crest of the Wave.* Ventura, California: Regal Books, 1983.

————. *Our Kind of People.* Atlanta: John Knox Press, 1979.

_____ . *Spiritual Power and Church Growth*. Altamonte Springs, Florida: Strang Communications, 1986.

_____ . *Your Church Can Be Healthy*. Nashville: Abingdon, 1979.

_____ . *Your Church Can Grow: Seven Vital Signs of a Healthy Church*. Ventura, California: Regal Books, 1976.

Walther, C. F. W. *The Proper Distinction Between Law and Gospel*. Saint Louis: Concordia, 1929(?).

Wesley, John. *The Works of John Wesley*, Vol. 1. Kansas City: Nazarene Publishing House, n.d.

Wright, J. Eugene. "Church Growth: Ultimate or Penultimate?" *The Christian Ministry* (January 1979): 11-15.

Other Selected Works

Aldrich, Joseph C. *Life-Style Evangelism*. Portland, Oregon: Multnomah Press, 1981.

Allen, Roland. *Missionary Methods: St. Paul's or Ours?* Grand Rapids: Eerdmans, 1962.

Baisden, Kenneth. "Testing for Spiritual Gifts: Sham, or Sure-Fire?" M.Div. Dissertation, Concordia Seminary, Saint Louis, Missouri, 1984.

Bonhoeffer, Dietrich. *The Cost of Discipleship*. New York: MacMillan, 1959.

Brock, Charles. *The Principles and Practice of Indigenous Church Planting*. Nashville: Broadman, 1981.

Chaney, Charles L. *Church Planting at the End of the Twentieth Century*. Wheaton, Illinois: Tyndale, 1982.

Chemnitz, Martin. *Justification: The Chief Article of Christian Doctrine*. Translated by J. A. O. Preus. Saint Louis: Concordia, 1985.

Christian Life Magazine, "Signs and Wonders Today." Wheaton, Illinois: Christian Life Magazine, 1983.

Cortright, Charles. "Church Growth and Its Implications for the Use of the Means of Grace in a Confessional, Liturgical Church," A paper presented at the Free Lutheran Conference of the Peninsula, San Mateo, CA, February 2, 1989.

Engstrom, Ted. *The Making of a Christian Leader*. Grand Rapids: Eerdmans, 1976.

Feucht, Oscar E. *Everyone a Minister*. Saint Louis: Concordia, 1981.

Fleming, Bruce C. E. *Contextualization of Theology, An Evangelical Assessment*. Pasadena: William Carey Library, 1980.

Fuller, Daniel P. *Gospel and Law: Contrast or Continuum?* Grand Rapids: Eerdmans, 1980.

Garlow, James L. *Partners in Ministry*. Kansas City, Missouri: Beacon Hill, 1981.

Gibbs, Eddie. *Church Growth Principles: What They Are and What They Mean*. Pasadena, Fuller Theological Seminary.

Goble, Philip E. *Everything You Need to Grow a Messianic Synagogue*. South Pasadena: William Carey Library, 1974.

Hale, J. Russell. *The Unchurched: Who They Are and Why They Stay Away*. San Francisco: Harper and Row, 1980.

Heck, Joel D. *Make Disciples: Evangelism Programs of the Eighties*. Saint Louis: Concordia, 1984.

Hoge, Dean R., and Roozen, David A. *Understanding Church Growth and Decline*. New York: Pilgrim, 1979.

Hubbard, David Allen. *What We Evangelicals Believe*. Pasadena: Fuller Seminary, 1979.

Huebel, Glenn. "The Church Growth Movement: A Word of Caution." *Concordia Theological Quarterly*, Vol. 50 (July-October, 1986): 165-181.

Hunter, Kent R. *Your Church Has Personality*. Nashville: Abingdon, 1985.

Kelly, Dean M. *Why Conservative Churches Are Growing*. San Francisco: Harper and Row, 1977.

Lindberg, Carter. "Pietism and Church Growth Movement in a Confessional Lutheran Perspective." *Concordia Theological Quarterly*, Vol. 52 (April-July, 1988): 129-148.

Maner, Robert. *Making the Small Church Grow*. Kansas City, Missouri: Beacon Hill Press, 1982.

Matthias, Elmer W. "This Lutheran Sees Value in Church Growth." *Concordia Journal* (March, 1984): 53-63.

Matzat, Don. *Inner Healing: Deliverance or Deception?* Eugene, Oregon: Harvest House, 1987.

Owen, Bert Lewis. "A Study of the Church Growth Movement." *The Cumberland Seminarian* (Spring, 1980): 3-41.

Parvin, Earl. *Missions USA*. Chicago: Moody Press, 1985.

Peters, Thomas J., and Waterman, Robert H. *In Search of Excellence*. New York: Warner Books, 1982.

Quebedeaux, Richard. *The New Charismatics II*. San Francisco: Harper and Row, 1976.

Reed, R. C. *The Gospel as Taught by Calvin*. Grand Rapids: Baker, 1979.

Reeves, Daniel R., and Jensen, Ronald. *Always Advancing: Modern Strategies for Church Growth*. San Bernardino: Here's Life Publishers, 1984.

Savage, John S. *The Apathetic and Bored Church Member.* Pittsford, New York: LEAD Consultants, Inc., 1976.

Schaller, Lyle E. *Hey, That's Our Church.* Nashville: Abingdon, 1978.

_____ . *Assimilating New Members.* Nashville: Abingdon, 1978.

_____ . *Growing Plans.* Nashville: Abingdon, 1983.

_____ . *The Small Church Is Different.* Nashville: Abingdon, 1982.

Scheiderer, Steven. "The Church Growth Movement: A Lutheran Analysis." STM Dissertation, Concordia Seminary, Fort Wayne, Indiana, 1985.

Schuller, Robert. *Your Church Has Real Possibilities!* Glendale: Regal Books, 1974.

Seifert, Donald. "An Evaluation of the Church Growth Movement." A paper delivered to the WELS California Pastor's Conference, January 26, 1981.

Stedman, Ray C. *Body Life.* Ventura, California: Regal, 1972.

Stott, John R. W. *Christian Mission in the Modern World.* Downers Grove, Illinois: Intervarsity Press, 1975.

Synan, Vincent. *The Holiness Pentecostal Movement in the United States.* Grand Rapids: Eerdmans, 1971.

Tillipaugh, Frank R. *The Church Unleashed.* Ventura, California: Regal Books, 1982.

Tippett, A. R. *Church Growth and the Word of God.* Grand Rapids: Eerdmans, 1970.

Towns, Elmer. *The Complete Book of Church Growth.* Wheaton, Illinois: Tyndale, 1983.

Wagner, C. Peter. *Your Church and Church Growth.* Pasadena: Fuller Evangelistic Association, 1982.

Waymire, Bob, and Wagner, C. Peter. *The Church Growth Survey Handbook.* Milpitas, California: Global Church Growth, 1984.

Wells, David F., and Woodbridge, John D. *The Evangelicals.* Nashville: Abingdon, 1975.

Wendland, Ernst H. "An Evaluation of Current Missiology." *Wisconsin Lutheran Quarterly,* Vol. 78 (April, 1981): 104-120.

_____ . "Church Growth Theology." *Wisconsin Lutheran Quarterly,* Vol. 77 (April, 1981): 104-120.